Amateurs at Arms

An Early American Society Book

The editors of *Early American Life,* the Society's official magazine, have checked this book for historical and, where possible, factual accuracy. Opinions and interpretations expressed within its pages have been left as written by the author. It is the objective of the Society to sponsor and recommend books that it feels have lasting value to persons interested in colonial and early American times—books that are both entertaining and enlightening.

                      Robert G. Miner
                      President and Editor of Publications

Amateurs at Arms

George Wunder

Stackpole Books

AMATEURS AT ARMS

Copyright © 1975 by George Wunder

Published by STACKPOLE BOOKS
Cameron and Kelker Streets
Harrisburg, Pa. 17105

All rights reserved, including the right to reproduce this book or portions thereof in any form or by any means, electronic or mechanical, including photocopying, recording, or by any information storage and retrieval system, without permission in writing from the publisher. All inquiries should be addressed to Stackpole Books, Cameron and Kelker Streets, Harrisburg, Pennsylvania 17105.

Library of Congress Cataloging in Publication Data

Wunder, George, 1912-
   Amateurs at arms.

   1. United States—History—Revolution, 1775-1783—Biography. I. Title.
E206.W86   973.3'092'2 [B]   75-28502
ISBN 0-8117-0096-8

Printed in the U.S.A.

CONTENTS

Preface   9

Acknowledgments   11

Days of Silver, Nights of Steel   12
  A law-abiding silversmith by day, Paul Revere daringly smuggles cannon from under the noses of British sentries by night.

The Man Who Loved the Law   14
  Ardent patriot though he is, John Adams, determined that the new American state shall not come into being on the shoulders of a lynch mob, exercises his utmost skill as a lawyer to defend the British soldiers involved in the Boston Massacre.

The Freshly Minted Widow   16
  Clutching the flintlock from the body of her fallen husband, Jonathan Harrington's widow vows to make the Redcoats pay for the death of her husband.

Art Is Long—Fame Is Fleeting   18
  John Trumbull, soon to become a noted painter of the American Revolution, enlists the aid of a British deserter in his dangerous mission of spying upon and drawing the enemy works guarding Boston.

The Leader Must Also Pay His Dues   20
  Believing that a man could not leave to others the grim details of supporting his convictions, Doctor Joseph Warren, firebrand of the Revolution, sacrifices his life for liberty in the fighting on Breed's Hill.

The Country Captain   22
  Captain William Delaplace, the British career officer in command of Fort Ticonderoga, winces as Colonel Ethan Allen attempts the civility due to a defeated enemy and consumes his rum at an awe-inspiring rate.

The Bookseller   24
  Bookseller Henry Knox, an armchair expert on artillery, puts his knowledge to the test when he transports the cannon needed to force Howe's evacuation of Boston from Fort Ticonderoga to Dorchester Heights.

The Opportunist   26
Captain Hugh Hill of Beverly, Massachusetts, and his fellow privateersmen, spurred by profit and patriotism, capture many a rich merchant prize in British home waters.

The Boy   28
Fifteen-year-old Joseph Plumb Martin, a recruit in the 5th Connecticut Line, is quickly disillusioned in his expectation of a speedy, painless patriot victory.

The Rash Commander   30
His early optimism dashed, Colonel Robert Magaw reluctantly accepts the grim necessity of surrendering 2800 men, together with great stores of munitions and war materiel, to the British forces encircling Fort Washington.

The Official Visitor   32
The guns of Fort Oranje on the Dutch island of St. Eustatius boom an answering salute to the Continental Navy's new armed brig, Andrew Doria, *thereby crowning the mission of Captain Isaiah Robinson, the brig's commander, with success.*

The Tradesman   34
An erstwhile hatter outrages the dignity of British Major General Richard Prescott by kidnapping him in his nightshirt.

The Propagandist   36
Embittered by desertions from Washington's troops, that perpetually angry man, Thomas Paine, excoriates the defectors in words that sting like a whip.

The Cattle Dealer   38
Double agent John Honeyman, posing as a drover, gets himself captured by Continental dragoons in order to relay the news of Trenton's vulnerability to General Washington.

The Fishermen   40
Colonel John Glover and the deep-sea fishermen of the Marblehead Regiment put their civilian skills to use in the vital mission of ferrying Washington's troops across the Delaware.

The Purchasing Agent   42
Under the guise of a legitimate export business, Hortalez et Cie (a front for the Bourbon kings of France and Spain) ships war materiel to the embattled colonies as directed by Benjamin Franklin's agent, Silas Deane.

The Besieged   44
The British hope to force the surrender of Fort Stanwix by holding the entire civilian population of the Mohawk Valley hostage to massacre by the Iroquois, but a clever bluff engineered by Benedict Arnold causes the Indian allies of the British to desert in droves, thereby saving the fort.

The Stubborn Man   46
Miffed by Congress's failure to recognize the military talents he has displayed at Bunker Hill, Trenton, and Princeton, Colonel John Stark remains aloof from the war until Burgoyne's push down Lake Champlain raises his hackles, and the sharpshooting woodsmen under his command make mincemeat of Burgoyne's Hessian forces.

The Legendary Hero   48
Peter Francisco, a six-foot-six, 250-pound adolescent, keeps the 10th Virginia as steady as a rock in the Battle of Brandywine.

The Loyal Opposition   50
Tory troops play a key role when Sir Henry Clinton's forces overwhelm Fort Montgomery, Rebel stronghold on the Hudson, but they are too late to link up with Burgoyne.

The Tactician   52
Colonel Thaddeus Kosciusko, Polish military engineer, wins the grudging admiration of Daniel Morgan for his design of the redoubts and entrenchments used by the sharpshooting Americans to decimate Burgoyne's forces at Saratoga.

The Inventor   54
Inventor David Bushnell succeeds in making the British look ridiculous, but fails in his objective of sinking the British fleet in the Delaware with floating mines.

The Teacher   56
Although the credentials he flaunts are improbable, Baron von Steuben succeeds in instilling military discipline in the Continental troops by using the elite training battalion under his command as an example.

The Listening Lady   58
Lydia Darrah, a demure Quaker lady whose home quarters Sir William Howe's adjutant general, overhears a plan for a surprise attack on Washington's main force at Whitemarsh in time to turn the tables on the British.

The Unexpecting Victor   60
Lieutenant Colonel William Smith, John Adams's son-in-law, is dismayed by the retreat of American forces at the Battle of Monmouth and overjoyed when the rout is brought to an end by Washington's reprimand of General Charles Lee, responsible for the debacle.

The Prisoner   62
Summary justice is meted out to a traitor by American captives on board the British prison ship Jersey.

The Bluffing Gambler   64
Colonel George Rogers Clark, with a strike force never larger than an outsize combat patrol, wins over the townspeople of the Indiana Territory and nonplusses the British.

The New Elite   66
The daring and successful assault on the British fort at Stony Point by American forces under General "Mad Anthony" Wayne and Colonel Richard Butler gives proof that the Continentals have become the equal of Britain's best.

The Unexpected Gunner   68
The use of artillery against the Iroquois by General John Sullivan's expeditionary force so terrifies the Indian allies of the British that they never again oppose American troops armed with artillery.

The Kindred Spirit   70
Count Casimir Pulaski, gallant Polish aristocrat and distinguished libertarian, is cut down by a sniper's round in the foolhardy frontal assault on the British fortifications at Savannah ordered by the Comte d'Estaing.

The Reckless Pragmatist   72
John Paul Jones may never have won the famous naval battle between the Bonhomme Richard *and the* Serapis *if William Hamilton, a regularly enlisted seaman under his command, hadn't thrown a grenade from a main yard of the American vessel into the powder magazine of the British warship.*

The Deadly Antagonists   74
The wily "Swamp Fox," Francis Marion, outwits Lord Cornwallis's daring cavalry commander, Colonel Banastre Tarleton.

The Inquisitive Lady   76
Sally Townsend, in whose home British officers are quartered, overhears a discussion of Arnold's plot to betray West Point.

The Turncoat's Turncoat   78
Under orders from General Washington, Sergeant Major John Champe risks his life by deserting the American ranks in a futile attempt to bring the traitor Benedict Arnold to justice.

The Spontaneous Heroes   80
At the Battle of Cowpens the crafty patriot general, Daniel Morgan, turns his undependable Militiamen into veritable tigers with a devious combination of flattery and cajolery.

The Night Rider   84
A British plot to capture Thomas Jefferson, Patrick Henry, and other key leaders of the American rebellion is foiled by Militia Captain Jack Jouette's breakneck predawn ride.

The Small Destroyers   82
Lord Cornwallis wins a pyrrhic victory over Colonel William Washington's Continental Dragoons at the Battle of Guilford Court House—a victory which occasions some sardonic humor among the wits of the British drawing room set.

The Mutineers   86
When there is a near breakdown of the food and clothing supply system in the middle of the most brutal winter of the war, one of the proudest brigades in the Continental Army, "Mad Anthony" Wayne's Pennsylvania Line, turns out its officers.

The Missionary   88
The young Count de Damas, a participant in the Battle of Yorktown, feels sure that the egalitarian ideals of the American Revolution will sweep his native France, but he does not realize the price he will have to pay when they do.

The Old Soldier   90
Battle-hardened Sergeant Joseph Plumb Martin recalls his days as a raw recruit while he observes the British surrender at Yorktown.

The Victors   92
As he watches General Washington take leave of his officers at Fraunces' Tavern, Alexander Hamilton dreams of an America governed by a new aristocracy under a constitutional monarchy.

The Reactivated Civilian   94
Mustered out of the service and on the road home, the veteran of the Regular Line unconsciously begins to think like a civilian.

PREFACE

In a younger, less sophisticated age, he was part of America's legend. Statues of him were erected, usually in bronze, and many a town square was so graced.

There he stood, legs rigid, heels planted firmly in the soil. Often he was shown rolling up a sleeve, musket in hand, while a coat draped with studied casualness over the grip of a tilted plow symbolized his turning from peaceful pursuits to the conduct of war. Invariably he was spare, lean-faced and firm of jaw, his eyes squinted in determination. Over the years, he gave America a comfortable feeling of security. It was understood that, in time of danger, the Yankee—instantly armed and instinctively competent—would always prove superior to any combination of "decadent" foreigners. He was the Minuteman!

But time changes people's attitudes. Over the course of years a sobering erosion took place. Historians delved, then embarrassedly referred to the number of recorded times the Minuteman simply walked away because his farm required attention, or the grim military exercises of the British had reminded him to consider the virtues of self-preservation. Military men, beribboned and coldly professional, commented clinically on his early aversion to close combat with the bayonet, his staggering ignorance of logistics and his penchant for electing his own officers, often resulting in popular figures (such as the local tavernkeeper) becoming regimental commanders.

The detractors would have been correct too, if only their basic premise had not been mistaken. They tried to judge the American Revolutionary soldier by the same standard they would use to evaluate the European military man. The mistake was in the fact that the Briton, Frenchman, Prussian, etc. was, if an officer, of the gentry, bound by tradition and the obligations of his caste to a rigid code of conduct. If a common soldier, he was a peasant, sullenly docile for the previous two millennia, perfectly adapted to being molded into an obedient automaton more terrified of the triangle and the lash than the enemy's volleys.

While these disciplined battalions were performing their deadly minuets on the battlefields of Europe, the English colonies in North America were producing a breed of men such as hadn't been seen since the best days of the Roman Republic. These Americans were of the same stripe as those grimly infuriated citizens who flung themselves against the Carthaginian armies until the bloody grounds were littered with Hannibal's elite.

Independent, obstinate as well, these Americans were descendants of the refugees and riffraff of Britain, Scotland, Ireland, and Germany; of Holland, Africa, and France. But supermen they were not! They were no more, nor less, courageous than their opponents. Their rank and file were frequently illiterate, largely ignorant of the greater implications of the contest in which they'd become involved. Moreover, they were unimpressed with military glory, and contemptuous of the soldiers' codes and customs. All in all, our Revolutionary War soldier was never anything but a civilian who'd been pushed around, didn't like it, and decided to push back!

It's true the colonists weren't complete innocents in a warring world. They, or their forebears, had come from Europe. Many had served in those rigid ranks. Some had served as colonial militia beside the very regiments of grenadiers and fusiliers they were now to oppose. In the war against the French for Canada and the West (1765), they'd behaved with a commendable amount of courage seasoned with a generous dash of insubordination. British commanders came to view their native auxiliaries with uneasiness. The scarlet-clad heirs of Marlborough were remarkably unsympathetic to a military system consisting largely of irregularly held musters, which were mostly an excuse for a barbeque, much swanking around in hand-me-down uniforms, and a retreat parade to the nearest tavern by all ranks.

Eventually the American did learn how to soldier, but without ever really becoming one. Like the practical farmer, merchant, fisherman, trapper that he was, he learned from his mistakes. He learned that, while sniping from cover was a valuable method of eliminating the enemy's officers, it was not effective for taking and holding ground, a shortcoming which the Minuteman's critics have always been eager to point out.

This unorthodoxy, though, did have a certain merit in an age when any departure from standard military doctrine was regarded as sacrilege. It kept the British off-balance, unable to function with their customary efficiency while the Americans slowly mastered winning tactics and realistic strategy a grim education taught by defeats. Eventually they gained the European-style disciplined steadiness which made them the equals of their formidable foe.

Angered by a system they no longer respected, nor willingly obeyed, the Revolutionary Americans set in motion a process which was to change the established order over much of the world, a process which—for better or worse—is still going on. It is not a coincidence that so many newer nations modeled their constitutions on the one forged in Philadelphia. Because of what they succeeded in doing, no government in the world today, no matter how completely it dominates its people, can afford to totally ignore what can happen if it angers its citizenry to the point where they are willing to set aside private affairs in favor of grave public concerns.

Confronted today with problems far different from those of the Revolutionary War era, many Americans feel little affinity with the first citizens of these United States. Perhaps it is too difficult to identify with those nobly stylized figures, pictured against elegantly formal battlefields. Perhaps the overenthusiastic embellishments of patriotic biographers have made them seem more legend than fact. Perhaps it is simply that most of us are the descendants of immigrants, with no tribal continuity linking us to those of our nation's earliest years.

Still, there is one common bond between today's 20th-century Americans and those rigid manikins in pigeon-spattered bronze, those somber faces eyeing us doubtfully from dark old oil paintings. We are—as they were—dedicated, card-carrying civilians. It is surely one of the remarkable facts about the American Revolution that, except for a handful of European professionals, idealists, and mercenaries, the magnificent British Army was driven out of its King's colonies by clerks and farmers, lawyers and fishermen!

How well those civilians learned the military skills can best be evaluated by the British surrenders at Saratoga and Yorktown. The soldiers of the crown were no pushovers. The royal armies eliminated there were composed of courageous, superbly trained troops, officered by people of enough competence who'd created a huge empire to serve their small island.

Probably no political revolt, with the exception of the French and Russian, has been so intently examined and appraised by as many historians as the American Revolution. Both its wise men and fools have been identified and the effects of their actions on the birth of this nation judiciously assessed. To restate the already well-known would seem pointless. There remains, however, a vast field of minor incidents—some of lasting significance, others of little moment and quickly forgotten—which, when taken together, offer further insight into the war. Here, I feel, is an opportunity to put together a sampling of events and incidents from the great revolt which will serve as reminders that those dimly glimpsed figures out of our national past were real flesh and blood and that they were, very much, in our meaning of the term, "concerned citizens."

It took all kinds of people to win the American War for Independence; not all of them served in the armed forces. Some were quiet, unassuming housewives whose mixture of curiosity and patriotism spurred them to eavesdrop on the conversations of British officers quartered in their homes and to pass on the military secrets gleaned thereby to the patriot forces. Others were shrewd businessmen who did not neglect their own profit as they negotiated with foreign governments and merchants to obtain the war materiel so necessary to the American victory. Likewise, the captains and crewmen of American privateers lined their own pockets at the same time they were harassing England's mercantile fleet and choking off the supply lines of British troops in America. But however mixed their motives may have been, the men and women involved in the incidents recounted in the following pages were all caught up in the most momentous event of the eighteenth century. Often amateurish, frightened, and confused, they rose to the occasion and coped with what historians would regard as the most significant instant of their lives, courageously, honorably, and with an imaginative regard for the welfare of those who would come after them.

ACKNOWLEDGMENTS

For invaluable help in recreating scenes and events from the Revolutionary War, I am indebted to Clyde Peters and Neil McAleer of Stackpole Books, whose aid and encouragement were crucial. For many of the incidents pictured, I am also obliged to the writers and editors of *American Heritage*, whose carefully researched pieces have kept alive so many authentic stories of the American Revolution. For the correctness of uniform and weapon, rank and organization, I am appreciative of several works—Harold Peterson's *The Book of the Continental Soldier* (1968), Stackpole Books, Harrisburg, Pennsylvania; Alan Kemp's *The British Army in the American Revolution* (1973) and *American Soldiers of the Revolution* (1972), Almark Publishing Co., Ltd., London; Charles Lefferts' *Uniforms of the American, British, French and German Armies in the War of the American Revolution, 1775-1783* (1971), We Inc., Old Greenwich, Connecticut; and Stephen Bonsal's *When the French Were Here* (1945), Kennikat Press, Fort Washington, N.Y. Numerous other supportive sources were also consulted.

DAYS OF SILVER, NIGHTS OF STEEL

The revolt of the British colonials began, as most revolutions do, with that first overt act as formalized as a chess game. At the moment an angry citizenry's resentment becomes revolt, the rebels are acutely aware of their lack of the tools with which to wage war. Before the governing authority can be openly challenged, men must be rallied, war materiel must be hoarded and a fighting machine created. An underground organization, however, requires nothing more than a handful of dedicated men.

The Royal officers of His Majesty's City of Boston, Colony of Massachusetts, suspected that behind the Provincials' Committees of Safety and Correspondence there was a clandestine cell which carried out the less respectable affronts to good order. They were quite right.

It would have been something of a shock, however, if they'd been aware that the chief agent of that secret service was the same silversmith, of high repute, whose elegantly designed works graced so many of their dining tables.

☆☆☆

In the shadow of the massive gun shed, Paul Revere froze, motionless against the wall, his grip tight on the butt of the cocked pistol. Behind him, in the shed's cavernous interior, there was no sound from his fellow agents. Mentally, he blessed the mist drifting in from the Charles River masking sight and sound in this Royal Artillery Depot, hard by the North Battery.

The sound which had immobilized Revere's working party was more distinct now. The sentry's heels thudded sharply on the brick walk with the cadence of the British soldier's slow march. Now he came into view just beyond the row of parked howitzers lined up across the yard. This British Army facility had been under surveillance by Revere's cell for some time. The American agent knew that the man was precisely on time.

The inflexible attitudes of the British Army were a great comfort to a man in his position, Revere reflected. The sentry was a gunner in the dark blue with red facings of the Royal Artillery. He marched with that rigid, manikinlike gait which European officers of the 18th century considered the mark of good discipline. It was likely that his fixed gaze couldn't have spotted any movement more than ten degrees to either side of his post. This was beneficial as it prevented him from noticing what dangled from the loading beam over Revere's head.

The sentry's back disappeared from view among the rows of supply sheds. He would be back in exactly seven minutes. There were no other sentry posts in this part of the depot. The British military refused to admit their apprehension over the public attitude by increasing the guard details.

Revere relaxed the grip on his pistol, and nodded to William Dawes just inside the shed's entrance. There was a whisper of sound as the rope tightened in the sheaves of the block and tackle. His schoolmaster's dignity forgotten, Abraham Holbrook, still gripping his pistol, grasped the guideline and the suspended brass cylinder dropped smoothly into the waiting wagon.

Dawes (the operator of a tannery) was quickly at Revere's side. "Got the cannon, Paul. Lots of other . . ."

Revere shook his head negatively, in a request for silence; the sentry would be back in four minutes now. He'd be approaching the gun shed. He couldn't help but see what was happening. With an underground agent's sure instinct, Revere knew that a departure from the prearranged plan would involve delay, discovery, and violence. A shot fired meant a bungled mission. He shook his head, his eyes still trained on the spot where the sentry would reappear.

With a shrug, the tanner motioned to the rest of his group. They put their combined shoulders to the cart. Like the block, it had been freshly greased. It rolled silently across the depot dock to where a barge had materialized out of the darkness. A gangway was hurriedly dropped into place and the loaded wagon manhandled aboard. With one minute to spare, Revere himself slipped aboard and the barge drifted silently out into the tide.

Next morning, a choleric Major Paddock of the Royal Artillery promised dire punishment to a bewildered sentry, knowing full well that he'd get the same shortly from General Gage. A complete battery of brass fieldpieces, fresh from the London gunfounder's yard, missing—only to reappear emplanted in the Rebel stronghold atop Breed's Hill not too far in the future.

However, before that time of final, overt defiance, there was other work for the Rebel underground. There was one matter of the North Battery's heavy guns coming to rest under the waters of a nearby pond, another of a somewhat destructive tea party. Perhaps, however, the clandestine group's major coup involved piecing together certain items of intelligence regarding British military activities in Boston, determining General Gage's intentions and properly estimating their importance.

Many years later, a poet was to romantically immortalize Paul Revere's name in the history of a new nation. It's likely, however, that he would have preferred that the credit for alerting the Rebel units in Lexington and Concord went to his unit's professional teamwork. After all, he'd been intercepted by a forewarned British patrol, composed entirely of officers. It had been his backup man, Dr. Samuel Prescott, who'd gotten through.

THE MAN WHO LOVED THE LAW

All too often when an outraged citizenry rebels and strikes out at its government, the first casualty is its own orderly society. The history of authority overthrown is one of "Revolutionary Justice," "Peoples' Courts," and the like, all quasi-judicial excuses for bloody mob vengeance. In a court where passion is the jury, the verdicts are apt to bear a certain similarity; "To the Block! To the Wall! To the Guillotine!" Only in the aftermath, when the fury has spent itself, does it occur to the rebel that the regime he has forged is already dishonored, no better than the oppression it replaced.

☆☆

John Adams had always been a thoughtful man. A lawyer, he loved the cool detachment, the impersonal logic of the law. A firm believer in the patriot cause, he'd still written articles in the Revolutionary press regretting its excesses. An attitude such as this did not make it easy to practice law in the City of Boston, Colony of Massachusetts.

He knew that everything he believed in was in jeopardy because of the bloody business in front of the Custom House. Five dead and six wounded, his townsmen all. The victims had provoked their own bloodying, but still the city—his city—was demanding revenge.

Nine British soldiers (only one an officer), facing a hysterical mob, howling for their heads. It must have been a confused nightmare. The soldiers dodging the barrage of snowballs, rocks, bricks, and sharp oyster shells, unable to hear Captain Preston's commands above the roar of the crowd. How far could even the ferocious discipline of the British Army be stretched?

If only there weren't so many of his fellow citizens blinded by passion, it would be a simple matter to establish that the military had acted under extreme peril of their lives, carrying out their duty. Unfortunately, the issues were more complex than that.

His cousin Sam, Dr. Warren, Hancock, the militant Revere—all the Sons of Liberty—were determined to use the incident to widen the breach between the colony and the government in London. To lawyer Adams it seemed an unsavory use of a tragedy, but he also realized that it was politically useful, one more in the long succession of incidents which had put the factions on a collision course. Within the foreseeable future there would be a confrontation. Already, the colonists were Englishmen in name only, their ties to the Crown in tatters. Well and good! But the casual sacrifice of nine poor, benighted Lobsterbacks was an unacceptable price, even if their own officers (with that fine contempt of the "other ranks" typical of the British aristocracy), were interested only in saving Captain Preston's hide.

There would be a new American state, but it must not come into being on the shoulders of a lynch mob. Its pretension would be a sleazy joke if its legal processes were less than civilized.

He noted that the grenadiers in the dock were watching him anxiously. He couldn't blame them for being frightened. They couldn't think they had the ghost of a chance of receiving a fair trial. The 29th Regiment of Foot was a symbol of the King's oppression to most of the city. There would be no defense from the Loyalists, terrified for their own skins. Of the four justices, three had tried frantically to resign, their obligation to the law ignored. Only grim old Chief Justice Oliver's firmness had kept them on the bench.

So there it was. His hotheaded friends, too emotionally blinded to realize it, but they and their proposed state were on trial as well. And such a shabby trial! The witnesses had already given evidence, twisted evidence, colored by their own passions. Mr. Adams's junior, Josiah Quincy, had posed his questions skillfully but the verdict was predictable. It was likely their new nation would come upon the world's stage with its hands already bloody.

And now it was time for the defense to present its case to the jury. John Adams, one day soon to help negotiate a peace treaty with England, to become an Envoy to the Court of St. James, and finally to become the new nation's second president, rose from his place and faced the justices. His voice was crisp, dispassionate: "M'Lords, I am for the prisoners at the bar."

14

THE FRESHLY MINTED WIDOW

When the moment of open revolt arrives, no matter how firmly the civilian has steeled himself, how remorselessly he's whipped his passions with remembered wrongs, it's always an instant of dreadful realization. Suddenly the stirring speeches, the itemized righteousness of the cause, even the euphoria of reordering his own destiny, become very fragile shields in the face of a new reality. It is his body, vulnerable and weak, that now stands exposed to the terrible instruments of lead and steel by which authority imposes its will. Now begins the bitter education of the revolutionary.

☆☆☆

Up until the moment when the cold taste of fear came to Jonathan Harrington's wife, it had all been fantasy, an exercise to stimulate the mind, a release from the routine of daily life in her village of Lexington, colony of Massachusetts, in the strictly ordered world of 1775. The long evenings of argument in John Buchman's tavern, the brave talk full of ringing determination suddenly became sickeningly real.

The sound of horses' hooves had awakened her. Still half asleep, she'd heard the mumble of indistinct voices calling to each other. She'd been confused at first, then—when she realized that Jonathan was up pulling on his clothes—she'd recognized what was being called out on the dark common. British troops were on the way, searching for arms.

She'd attempted a protest as Jonathan took down the fine French flintlock his grandfather had brought over from Cornwall. Preoccupied with slinging powder horn and shot bag about his person, her husband hadn't seemed to hear her.

Outside, he'd been joined by their neighbors. From their bedroom window, she'd watched as the men assembled on the green. Faintly, she could hear the voice of Captain Parker, the Minuteman commander, trying to organize by cajoling them into some sort of military formation. The wait had seemed endless. Then, incredibly, it had been over. The Minutemen dispersed, some back to their beds, the more fiery to Buchman's. Jonathan had crawled back under the covers, promising strong vengeance on the idiot who'd get a man out of bed in the night on a fool's errand.

Her relief had been short-lived. In the morning, there had been another alert; this time, the real thing. The Minutemen had lined up on the Green, thirty-eight in all, according to one eyewitness. When the King's troops had marched into the village, she'd been petrified with terror at first. Then, she'd rationalized, surely the men would act like what they were—civilians. They were peaceful, God-fearing men with no business opposing hundreds of professional soldiers.

She'd watched, along with the other wives, as a British officer cantered out ahead of the column of grenadiers. She couldn't hear his words, but she knew what he must have said. It should have been enough to send those silly countrymen back to their families where they belonged.

Incredibly, it hadn't worked that way at all. They were still there. The Redcoat ranks were still facing them, rigid and without emotion. Then the unthinkable happened. She'd heard the officer's voice faintly in the distance. The bayonetted muskets leveled with machinelike precision. The volley seemed to shred every nerve in her body. When she opened her eyes, they had an unbelieving look in them.

There was a blue haze of gunpowder drifting in front of the British files. The scattered bodies lay very still. She was vaguely conscious of Minutemen—some without their weapons—running, limping, stumbling away. Then she saw Jonathan. He still had his fowling piece. It dangled casually from a limp arm. He was walking slowly, too slowly! She opened her mouth, but her cry died unborn. The red stain spreading so rapidly across his shirt front was simply not believable. She never knew if he saw her. His eyes stared blankly as ever so slowly he pitched to his knees and died, face down in the dirt.

Crouched beside her husband's body, her own racked with sobs, Jonathan Harrington's widow was dimly aware of the British troops falling in on the Concord road. The officer who'd ordered the grenadiers to fire sat on his horse quite near, calmly watching the columns move out. She couldn't know that he was Major Pitcairn of the British Marines, second in command of this search-and-destroy mission, a decent man, too professional to take any pride in this cheap victory over bumpkins.

Of one thing she was sure: she *hated* him. Even though she seemed to be numb, she was conscious that part of her mind was functioning coldly and clearly. Independent of her will, she was realizing that the British troops would be returning eventually. There was no haven for them, save Boston. She knew the routes they'd have to use. Quite calmly, she picked up Jonathan's flintlock.

ART IS LONG–FAME IS FLEETING

At the onset, revolutions are heady stuff. Among intellectuals they're apt to induce a glorious semantic binge. Phrases like "foiling oppressors," "casting off chains" and "creating brave new worlds" creep into ordinary conversations. This causes many parlor idealists to fling themselves rashly into the realities of armed conflict to their own discomfort and the annoyance of more pragmatic rebels.

A few find this new environment to their liking and achieve a ruthlessness which their less high-minded colleagues see as bloodcurdling. Most, fortunately for their causes, find the ugly necessities of armed rebellion uncomfortable. There is general relief when they decide to limit their participation to writing stimulating letters to each other.

☆☆

This was a damned humiliating position for a patriot and Harvard man. If the possibility of its leading to an aide-de-camp's post under General Washington, himself, hadn't been the motivation, he—John Trumbull—student and dabbler in art, would never have accepted an assignment involving his crawling around in the mud and high grass just beyond Boston Neck.

When he and his fellow scholars had enthusiastically endorsed the noble revolt against tyranny and marched forth to place themselves in the forefront of the struggle for liberty, he hadn't imagined he'd be expected to be sent on a mission better suited to a rascally spy. However, the commander in chief wanted accurate drawings of the British works guarding this approach to the city. At least they'd recognized his talent, even if they'd ignored that his father, governor of Connecticut, was a known Rebel sympathizer, thereby making son John doubly liable to the hangman's rope if he were taken. At twenty, young Trumbull preferred to enjoy the coming glorious utopia rather than be one of its first martyrs.

It was a sickening moment when he heard the rustle of grass behind him. A reluctant about-face—to find himself facing a British grenadier—wasn't reassuring. The two crouched in the grass, staring at each other in horror. The soldier assayed an uncertain smile. This startled Trumbull into inspecting the man. Oddly, the Redcoat was without his crested brass and fur hat, his uniform was askew and his breath smelled like a waterfront tavern after a press gang had cleared it out.

The man was recognizably drunk. Even as Trumbull was digesting this fact, the soldier lifted a grimy finger to his lips and winked conspiratorially. Then he furtively inspected the distant jumble of earthworks and gun positions at the city's perimeter. Satisfied, he sighed with relief, and from his canteen helped himself to a generous gulp of what smelled like rum of a character unknown to Harvard students. Trumbull realized that the grenadier had to be a deserter. He was also a reprieve from the peril making the artist nervous.

Drunk or not, the soldier would be familiar with the British defenses. He'd probably defected from the nearby trenches himself. Young Trumbull whipped a sheet of paper and a charcoal stick from a leather portfolio. The topography of the Neck was already sketched in. Bleary-eyed, the Englishman still recognized it. Sternly, the reconnaissance artist bombarded him with questions, intermixed with threats of how the savage colonials treated the persons of uncooperative deserters. The grenadier was knowledgeable and anxious to please.

Then, in the parlor of the Craigie House in Cambridge—Washington's headquarters—a staff officer inspected Trumbull's map, pronounced himself impressed and spoke favorably of that aide's post. Trumbull somberly contemplated a future of physical discomforts and gruesome dangers. With becoming humility, he declared himself unworthy.

A talented artist, John Trumbull returned to his studio and enjoyed a long career of painting the American Revolution. His canvases are noteworthy for their nobly idealized subjects and their complete lack of vulgar realism.

THE LEADER MUST ALSO PAY HIS DUES

They were mostly responsible men, the early leaders of what was to become the American Revolution. As business or professional people, they'd been conscious of their duty to their society, supposedly aware of the consequences that would result from the political trauma they were creating. It was a serious business and they thought they knew it.

It had been only after reasoned commitment that they'd sent their couriers galloping over the turnpikes of the northern colonies, carrying the call to arms which produced the ragtag army of militiamen now squatting in remarkably unmilitary disarray on the high ground beyond the city of Boston. Perhaps it was their lack of ordered pomp, their obvious vulnerability, which made it so evident that this army was a gathering of pathetic civilians.

☆☆☆

Of all the Committee of Safety, Doctor Joseph Warren had been the most eager to bring about an open confrontation with the authorities of the crown. He'd been among the first to realize that the only ultimate result of their plans could be freedom from Great Britain.

He'd also known that this liberty would carry an incidental cost in blood, lives, and property. As a mature man of affairs, he'd been sure he was prepared to accept that responsibility. Still the fact that bloodshed was now inevitable had chilled him. Perhaps the feeling for humanity which had led him to the practice of medicine, long dulled by his violent political concerns, had reasserted itself. At any rate, he was now painfully aware that these men and boys awaiting the inevitable British reaction to their challenge were so assembled because of his influence.

With its customary efficiency, Revere's spy network had interpreted the British troop preparations and notified the Committee of the impending assault. Now the impetuous firebrand, Doctor Joseph Warren, faced his own private confrontation. Very shortly now, soldiers half a world from home would deliver the lives the King's shillings had purchased. More painfully, men he knew, men of New England who were on the crests of those hills because he'd so willed it, would die as well. With all his heart he believed that he'd made the correct decision. Still, he faced an obligation with no options for an honorable man. He must join his friends in the trenches.

The Committee had voted him the rank of major general, but he'd had enough of giving orders. In his embroidered waistcoat, with a borrowed musket, he'd come into this fight as a volunteer. A man could not leave to others the grim details of supporting his convictions.

They were coming again now. Doctor Warren could only numbly regret that such human courage should be so grotesquely spent. The slope of Breed's Hill was already obscenely littered with scarlet-clad bodies. The ranks of the grenadiers were thinner now, their colors ripped by shot, stained by battle. It seemed to Joseph Warren that there was a macabre beat to the drums sounding the charge. Perhaps it was because he was beyond exhaustion, but he had the odd fantasy that the drummers were masked executioners rather than fresh-faced boys.

This time the British were not to be denied. They were in the trenches. Out of ammunition, cursing Americans were using their muskets as clubs in a wild melee. Enraged by their losses and humiliation, the grenadiers were wielding their bayonets with ruthless efficiency. Warren had a last round in his weapon. He couldn't bring himself to use it. Would his noble aims be served by one more useless death?

A grenadier, his face a mask of fury, lunged at him with a bloody bayonet. Warren fended it off. Howling curses, the Britisher careened past him. The doctor didn't look around at the sound of the high-pitched scream which came an instant later. His subconscious mind made the clinical observation that he was unable to think coherently. Stumbling, numb, he scrambled to the parapet of the trench.

It was almost as though he'd kept an appointment; he even recognized the hatless British captain a few feet away. With startling clarity he recalled that they'd once been fellow dinner guests in the home of a Boston shipowner. The last thing he ever saw was the spurt of flame from the officer's pistol.

THE COUNTRY CAPTAIN

A society in crisis, especially one as egalitarian and totally civilian in its attitudes as that of the English North American colonies, is apt to find its leaders among those whose talent for command would otherwise have remained unrecognized. The American Revolution gave birth to more than its share.

Oddly, it had been the boundary dispute between New York and New Hampshire which had demonstrated the similarity in qualifications required to be either a successful tavern brawler or respected military leader. The ill-advised attempts of New York sheriffs to extend their authority to the mountains known as the "Hampshire Grants" had met with determined opposition from the local timbermen, trappers, and farmers. These worthies had naturally turned for guidance to a hulking, ham-fisted backwoodsman whose dedication to violent solutions was already noteworthy. The Yorkers—harried back to Albany in a number of humiliating fashions—quickly learned, as the British would shortly, that Ethan Allen was a formidable foe.

☆☆

Captain William Delaplace was an unhappy man. As the commanding officer of Fort Ticonderoga, dominating the portage between Lakes George and Champlain, he'd not only suffered the misfortune of having his stronghold overrun by a mob of ferocious madmen led by a cursing, roaring giant for whom nothing in his previous military career had prepared him, but the ninety gallons of rum stored in the magazine below for his personal use was being consumed before his eyes at an awe-inspiring rate.

Suddenly, he was spun around to face Colonel Ethan Allen, an imposing figure under any circumstances. Now, with a huge mug gripped in a hairy fist, he was downright intimidating. The fact that he was attempting that civility to a defeated enemy regarded as proper etiquette by 18th-century military men somehow made him even more terrifying. His teeth bared in what he fondly assumed to be a cordial smile, the Yankee backwoodsman thrust the mug into the Briton's hand.

Delaplace shuddered. The mug contained a lethal local mixture of rum and hard cider known as a "Stonewall" to the indigenous population. It was not a potion for men with delicate sensibilities. The British captain reflected sadly that his fortress had been taken by surprise, with only a few wild shots fired haphazardly by his befuddled sentries. Now he was being intimidated into joining in the celebration of his own military disgrace.

Under Allen's benevolent eye, Delaplace sipped cautiously, speculated hopelessly that since his conqueror had already consumed several of the concoctions without falling on his face, he was probably immortal. This view was strengthened when the American seized his arm, guided him firmly into his own private office. There, Allen seated himself at the desk, selected paper and quill and proceeded to write.

Signing his effort with a flourish, Allen presented it to the Briton. Delaplace was not visibly enchanted to find himself holding a formal requisition for his rum and calling for the Committee of Correspondence of Connecticut to pay its fair value in some indefinite future with some unspecified currency.

The British captain's attention was diverted from the dubious document by the entrance of the other American colonel. Delaplace sourly contemplated his own five years in grade and wondered if these rebels gave field rank to any of their people who happened to be literate. He'd heard the second Yankee colonel addressed as "Arnold." Unlike Allen, the fellow wore a splendid uniform and his military bearing had been impeccable. Delaplace was puzzled by the fact that the conquering troops seemed to regard Arnold with a mixture of frivolity and contempt. The Englishman had the uneasy feeling that the saturnine Arnold was considerably deadlier than Allen.

Arnold was reading aloud a list for Allen's benefit, obviously an inventory of the materiel captured. No less than a hundred cannon, several mortars, three howitzers, one hundred stands of small arms, and a huge quantity of ball, powder, flints, wagons, and other military stores. Arnold announced that he was dispatching the list by courier at once to his superiors, the Massachusetts Committee of Safety. Allen retorted that he wouldn't care if Arnold sent his damned list to the emperor of Russia.

Dolefully, Delaplace drained his "Stonewall." The list brought home to him that his ninety gallons of rum were the least of the losses suffered by Great Britain through him.

He was right. Later, General Henry Knox (chief of the American artillery) was, on General Washington's own orders, to haul that massive assortment of hardware over snow-covered, frozen roads through the Berkshires. Set up on Dorchester Heights with their muzzles menacing Boston, they were to play an important part in persuading General Howe to evacuate that seat of rebellion.

THE BOOKSELLER

To the professional soldier, one of the more humbling frustrations to be faced when the civilian society he is supposed to police revolts, is the startling emergence of military skills among its lately docile citizenry. The British command was to find this especially so, as an officer corps began to form among the rabble of American colonial militiamen. Many of the merchants and lawyers who made their appearances with the Rebel forces investing Boston were to prove to be pompous frauds, to whom their posts were status symbols and opportunities to posture in fanciful uniforms. Their incompetence was to cost the new American Army dearly. Others, however, were to demonstrate a considerable native talent and an ability to learn from experience. Such a man was General Washington's newly appointed Chief of Artillery, General Henry Knox.

☆☆

Hannibal had been forced to cope with a somewhat similar problem, Henry Knox recalled. Among the benefits of operating a bookstore was that one got to read the merchandise. For many years, long before British troops began crowding the streets of Boston, he'd spent every free moment reading avidly. Military histories had always fascinated him, especially the development and uses of artillery. An enthusiastic gunner with a Boston militia battery, Henry Knox was an armchair expert on big guns.

It had been this expertise that impressed Washington in those first heady days of besieging Boston's British garrison. The new Congress had authorized the commander in chief to appoint officers. In a nation of blind men, the one-eyed man is king so, somewhat to the surprise of both, Washington had designated the bookseller his First Artilleryman.

Perhaps it was the example of long-dead captains immortalized in his books which animated Henry Knox, but overnight he'd become a daring, resourceful artillery tactician. When Washington had decided it would be unwise to attempt to drive General Sir William Howe from the city without a greater advantage in firepower, the captured cannon at Fort Ticonderoga were an obvious solution.

That was why Henry Knox was comparing a fresh snowfall with the weather conditions which had harassed a Carthaginian two millennia ago. True, the Berkshires weren't the Alps, but the logistical problem was similar. Fifty-nine cannon, ranging from light fieldpieces to heavy mortars, had to be manhandled through the hills to his waiting gunners, already digging emplacements on the crest of Dorchester Heights commanding Boston and its harbor.

There had already been delays. The scows bringing some of the heaviest guns down Lake George had sunk. It had been sheer luck that the accident happened in shallow water. Now he'd gotten as far as Great Barrington, and the roads were icy traps.

Outside Boston, Washington fretted. General Howe, replacing the amiable General Gage, might elect to attack. The Virginia planter's raw units could well disintegrate under siege.

The Commanding General found himself listening with some interest, as the clatter of hooves and a murmur of voices outside indicated that a dispatch rider had arrived. An aide brought the message to him. Then and there began a friendship and a mutual trust between the plantation owner and the bookseller which would last even beyond the day they would bid each other farewell in Fraunces' Tavern in New York years later.

The message was brief. Knox had obtained from General Schuyler, the New York commander, eighty-two yoke of oxen with sleds, and drovers. The firepower to drive Sir William Howe from Boston would be emplaced within the week.

THE OPPORTUNIST

An upheaval in society as drastic as a revolution always presents opportunities for profit and advancement. The profiteer and the ambitious demagogue make dependable appearances at such times. Even more common is the practical patriot, the fortunate individual who can practice his political conviction and his business acumen simultaneously. The era of the American Revolution was one well-suited to these doubly-talented men. It was an age when nations made use of an odd form of legalized piracy, privateering, to harass their sea-going enemies. Armed with "Letters of Marque"—licenses to prey upon enemy shipping—the masters and seamen of the colonial merchant marine found this method of warfare vastly preferable to service in the infant Congressional Navy, where the pay was poor and the discipline harsh.

☆☆☆

The American privateer *Pilgrim*, with Captain Hugh Hill of Beverly, Massachusetts commanding, had enjoyed a profitable cruise. Hill had realized from the onset that the prizes would be richest in the British home waters, where the trade routes of that maritime empire converged. His haul had been so handsome that most of his crew had been detailed as prize crews to sail the captured vessels into L'Orient, France.

The *Pilgrim* had been only a few hours out of the French port itself. Hill was already dressed in his best shore-going finery, as befitted a prosperous mariner. Then, the lookout had spotted a distant sail, barely visible across the sunlit Bay of Biscay. It was made out to be a small lugger, flying the British ensign. Even with his skeleton crew, Hill found it too tempting a tidbit to ignore. The Portuguese flag he was flying at the time enabled him to go close without arousing suspicion. It was when he'd broken out American colors that he discovered he had a hellcat by the tail.

Now, both vessels were badly damaged and, insult added to injury, the astonishingly large crew of the Britisher had adopted the privateersman's favorite tactic: Grappling hooks arching from the Britisher's deck had locked the two hulls together. Then, cutlasses slashing, boarders had come swarming through the American nets, to close in a wild melee with the Rebel seamen on the *Pilgrim*'s splintered and bloody decks. That was when an outraged Captain Hill had hurled his own considerable bulk into the brawl. He'd succeeded in rallying his wavering crew and, in the end, the English lost heart. It had been a hard day for them, too. They'd retreated in good order, cutting their own grapples as they went. Neither side was in the mood for further violence. The vessels had parted, each firing a face-saving small-arms' fusillade across the widening open water between them.

Captain Hill was an articulate man, his vocabulary enriched in the seaports of the world. He now commented emphatically on the lack of moral fiber sadly evident among a people capable of sending forth a boatload of thugs camouflaged as a helpless cargo coaster. The *Pilgrim*'s bosun, approaching with a report on casualties and damage, paused to listen in reverent admiration.

Eventually Captain Hill exhausted his repertoire of derogatory characterizations and turned his attention to the waiting bosun. "A damned customs cutter, Davey boy! Good thing we're cutting loose from the British bastards. They're a devious people and addicted to sharp practice. Now, run up that Portuguese flag again and let's be on our way."

THE BOY

It is not infrequently that revolts, holding the first advantage by virtue of their surprise element, enjoy an initial, lulling success, only to have it dissipated by reverses as the governing establishment recovers its poise and exercises its superior organization. This is the first acid test for the revolutionary. Inevitably there will be many for whom the shock of unmasked power is too great. They will discreetly vanish to await the outcome. How well the remainder face up to the grim reality of war in which they are outmanned, outgunned and outgeneraled, as well as branded as traitors without the rights of recognized belligerents, will largely determine the fate of their cause. This was particularly so with the American Rebels who, after the British evacuation of Boston, confidently expected an easy victory and an early birth of their scarcely visualized new nation.

☆☆

Joseph Plumb Martin was fifteen years old. He was also a raw rookie, newly recruited by Captain Samuel Peck into the 5th Connecticut Line at Milford. Like most colonial teenagers, he knew how to handle a gun and was an appalling optimist. Beyond that, his soldierly qualities were awesomely absent. The shortages which were to bedevil the Americans had not yet become epidemic. The 5th Connecticut was well-quartermastered. Joseph was issued a uniform, musket, bayonet, cartouche box, blanket, knapsack, and canteen.

Now he felt every inch a soldier as his unit swung at route step through the rain on a muddy Long Island road. Its orders were to join in contesting the drive by General Sir William Howe, striking out from the beachhead he'd established, and driving toward Manhattan Island, thus to seal off the mouth of the Hudson River.

Young Martin's regiment had scarcely arrived in New York before it was ordered to cross to Brooklyn, as reenforcement for General Israel Putnam's 9,000 men holding high ground against the massive pressure of the British Regulars and masses of newly-arrived, superbly disciplined Hessians.

The Connecticut infantrymen knew that the enemy was somewhere immediately ahead of them. At first excitement had kept them from noticing, but now they were becoming aware that they were cold, wet, and hungry. Young Joe was quick to discover that his complaint was not unique. There seemed to be a general feeling that Captain Peck, in picturing a pleasant stroll through picturesque Long Island, with the terrified Lobsterbacks in panic-stricken flight before them, had been less than candid. It seemed that the British morale hadn't been completely shattered by the evacuation of Boston after all. There were even a couple of morose malcontents who darkly speculated on the possibility that final victory might take longer than the five months they'd signed up for.

The men fell silent as the regimental sergeant major strode alongside the column, briskly threatening bodily harm to any misbegotten offspring of a brief dalliance between a farmer's slut and a passing pig drover, who took off on any unauthorized foraging expeditions.

Once past the snarling noncom, there was a flurry of muttered resentment by Martin's squadmates. Civilians to the core, these independent rookies were not impressed by arbitrary orders from a total stranger who didn't sound like a God-fearing credit to his community in the first place.

Eventually, the regiment was halted in a large meadow. Young Martin never knew who first raised the rumor that the barn, dimly seen through the sheets of rain, was filled with corn. The sergeant major's unreasonable attitude was dismissed contemptuously in view of the fact that cornmeal was the principal ingredient of johnnycakes, peerless material for stuffing empty stomachs.

Moments later, Joseph Plumb Martin was one of the party of volunteers creeping through the wet grass, utilizing a line of trees for cover and reaching the barn undetected. Peering in through the barn doorway, the boy recognized great stacks of bagged grain. There was also a hoarse voice which profanely advised him to leave before he attracted the Lobsterbacks down on them all.

With a shock the boy realized that hidden in the gloom were a score or more men, American stragglers from the fighting. The men of the 5th Connecticut were obscenely advised to find their own funk holes.

Young Martin's complaining stomach and his encounter with the deserters had preoccupied him, but now he became aware of a new sound. A sporadic rumbling, counterpointed by a sharp crackling, needed no interpretation. Uncertainly, the boy retreated to the door. The other Connecticut men were already outside. They stared—unbelieving. There were scattered groups of men hurrying across the open ground—away from the sounds of battle. The boy suddenly became aware that he was trembling. He knew those stumbling running men were rebels. The fantasies born at Boston were dying here in the rain.

A sudden blow to the side of his head nearly knocked him down. The enraged sergeant major was swinging his fists freely, driving his men before him. There were shouted orders from mounted officers, curses from the confused, milling men. Then, somehow, Joseph found himself back on the road, part of a stream of hurrying men. General Putnam's holding force was in full retreat. Only a rear guard of Maryland and Delaware Regulars saved a rout. The boy knew the tactic from his lost youth. Soldiers had a different name for it, but they were running away.

Joseph Plumb Martin hoped that his mates would think the moisture on his cheeks was rain. He supposed it would be a long time before he could swagger home in triumph as Captain Peck had promised.

THE RASH COMMANDER

There is no substitute for experience, and one of the hardest virtues for the new leaders of a revolution to learn is patience. For the new officer corps of the Continental Army it was very difficult. The early victories, Boston and Ticonderoga, had made them overconfident. Their confidence was jolted with the defeats on Long Island, the near-cutting-off of Manhattan, and the disaster at White Plains. Morale was devastated. To some disheartened senior officers of the American cause it had seemed that a victory—any victory, at whatever cost—was imperative. In view of the fact that Washington's army was a shambles whose only means of survival would be by escaping across the Hudson into New Jersey, the planning of such a miracle could only be termed foolhardy.

☆☆☆

Colonel Robert Magaw hoped he gave an appearance of calm assurance, even though the men of his command were well aware that Fort Washington, their improvised stronghold at the northern tip of Manhattan Island between the Hudson and Harlem rivers, was in dire peril.

When he and General Nathanael Greene had argued with a doubtful General Washington that the makeshift warren of log barricades, huts, and trenches could tie down Sir William Howe and his formidable regiments of British Regulars and Hessian mercenaries, what was now almost certain had seemed to them only a remote possibility.

The British had moved with professional competence. Lord Cornwallis had moved into a blocking position to the east. Lord Percy had taken his objective to the south with ease. Only north of Fort Washington, where Hessian General von Knyphausen was maneuvering for position, was there any dim hope of escape. There, Magaw's best units, Pennsylvania and Virginia riflemen, were in a firefight with the crack German *jaegers* under Colonel Johann Rall, trying to hold open a retreat corridor.

The slackening sounds of combat from that direction suggested that even such a remote possibility was rapidly vanishing.

A high-pitched whistle, followed by the collapse of a section of dirt and log parapet reminded the colonel of another unpleasant reality. The British had moved no less than sixteen batteries of artillery by barge past his guns and emplaced them on the east bank of the Harlem River, while from time to time the Royal Navy frigate *Pearl* dropped a shot or two into the fort to remind him that it was holding station on the Hudson side.

The colonel's gloomy mental exploration of the trap he'd talked himself into was interrupted by voices shouting his name. He turned to see a pair of soldiers helping another to enter by way of one of the cannon embrasures. As Magaw hurried toward them, he noted that the man was wounded. From his uniform, it could be seen that he was a sergeant with a Pennsylvania regiment. The man's voice was a hoarse croak, but his grasp of the situation in his sector north of the fort was precise. Magaw's last illusion died.

The fighting had been intense. The Hessian commander had sent *jaeger* sharpshooters in ahead of his grenadiers. In the duel between expert riflemen, the Americans had gained the upper hand, but the volume of fire was overheating their rifle barrels and depleting their stores of powder and ball. When Colonel Rall moved up his grenadiers, the frontiersmen's inherent weakness became decisive. For them, reloading was a slow, careful process. Their assortment of tomahawks, hunting knives and the like were no match for the Hessian grenadiers' bayonets, already possessed of a fearsome reputation earned in the recent Rebel defeats.

The Continental colonel leaned wearily against a gun carriage. His command was isolated. They could neither escape northward, nor could he cherish any forlorn hope of reenforcements from Washington's broken Army reaching him through the collapsed corridor. Further resistance simply meant useless slaughter. A cold bitterness gripped him as he realized that 2,800 men, among the best in the American Army, together with great stores of munitions and war materiel, were about to fall into the enemy's hands. He recognized the feeling blotting out all other emotions. It was remorse.

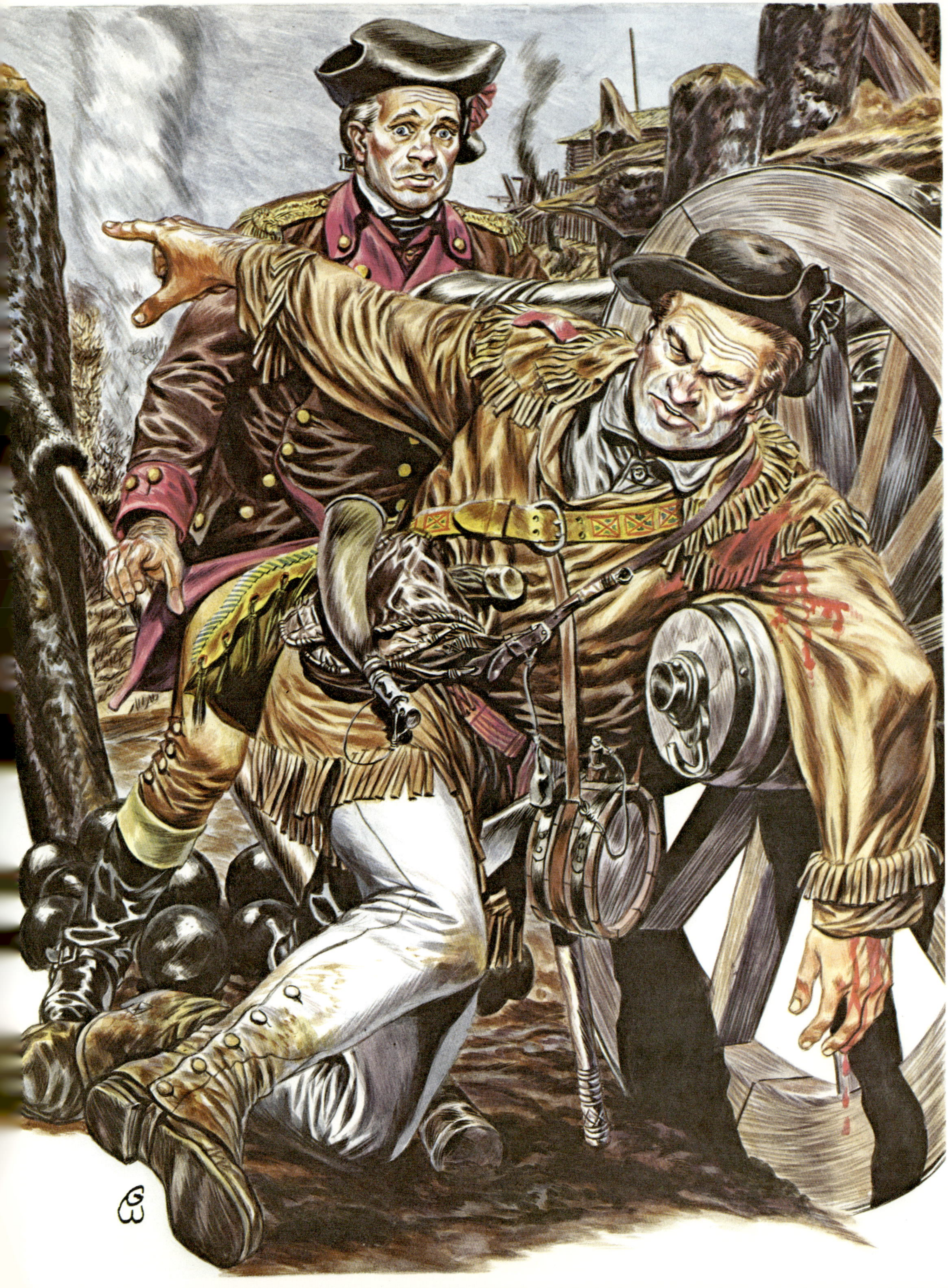

THE OFFICIAL VISITOR

To a revolutionary government, a matter of vital importance is its recognition by other states. Upon it depends the ability to conduct foreign affairs, make treaties and alliances, agree on trade, and regularize the status of its ships and citizens abroad. Of this, the American Congress was well aware.

The Dutch island of St. Eustatius was no unknown port of call to Yankee seamen. Long before the quarrel between Britain and her North American colonies had broken into the open, Oranjestad, its principal harbor, had been a point of transshipment from European flagships to American bottoms for illicit cargoes of everything from smuggled cannon to tea.

☆☆☆

To many of the sailors of the Continental Navy's new armed brig, *Andrew Doria*, she must have been a familiar sight. To the brig's commander, Captain Isaiah Robinson, she was something more. He had sailed under orders of the Marine Committee of the Congress with instructions to pick up a cargo of combat hardware awaiting him there. From the Secret Committee of the Congress, he had additional orders. The Congress had just officially signed the Declaration of Independence. As a matter of fact, he had a copy in the *Doria*'s strongbox for presentation to the Dutch governor.

Benjamin Franklin's Secret Committee was painfully aware that the document would be meaningless unless other nations recognized its validity. Robinson's mission was to coax a ceremonial gesture from the Dutch which could be taken to constitute acceptance of the flag he flew. From the *Andrew Doria*'s gaff, the new Grand Union flag of the United States rippled smartly in the wind.

Robinson balanced easily on his quarterdeck as the brig lost way, her topsails aback. A clatter and a splash signalled that her anchor was in the water. Scurrying to keep up with the barked orders of the bosuns, her seamen clewed up the spreads of new, white canvas. Robinson wanted no doubt in anyone's mind but that his brig was a proper naval vessel of the United States. The last line was no sooner secured than her saluting guns spoke.

At steady intervals, she would fire a thirteen-gun salute in honor of her host, the Dutch Republic. How that courtesy was returned meant the success or failure of the *Doria*'s mission.

Robinson knew that the Dutch governor was Johannes de Graaff. The previous governor had been removed when indignant British protests to The Hague over his favoritism toward American shipping reached embarrassing proportions. Now, de Graaff would have to make his pressured decision. The American captain waited with considerable interest to see how he would handle it.

The dirty whisp of smoke from the thirteenth shot was whipped from the cannon's mouth by the brisk wind. Fort Oranje seemed very close in the clear, warm sunshine. Then a patch of smoke blossomed, seemingly white against the fort's gray ramparts. The flat thud of its sound followed across the waters of the roadstead, as the answering salute began.

Robinson was aware that every man aboard his brig was counting the shots along with him. He wondered whether or not they realized the salute's significance. Eleven times the dull thump echoed, before the fort's guns fell silent. Robinson sighed, grinned at the diplomatic legalism. De Graaff had returned his salute, while still leaving himself a defense against the enraged protests of the British, sure to come. How well he'd succeeded was evident from the obvious fury of the English officers on the quarterdeck of the British sloop moored nearby.

Briskly, Captain Robinson called for his gig. He had a report to put aboard the first homeward-bound blockade runner.

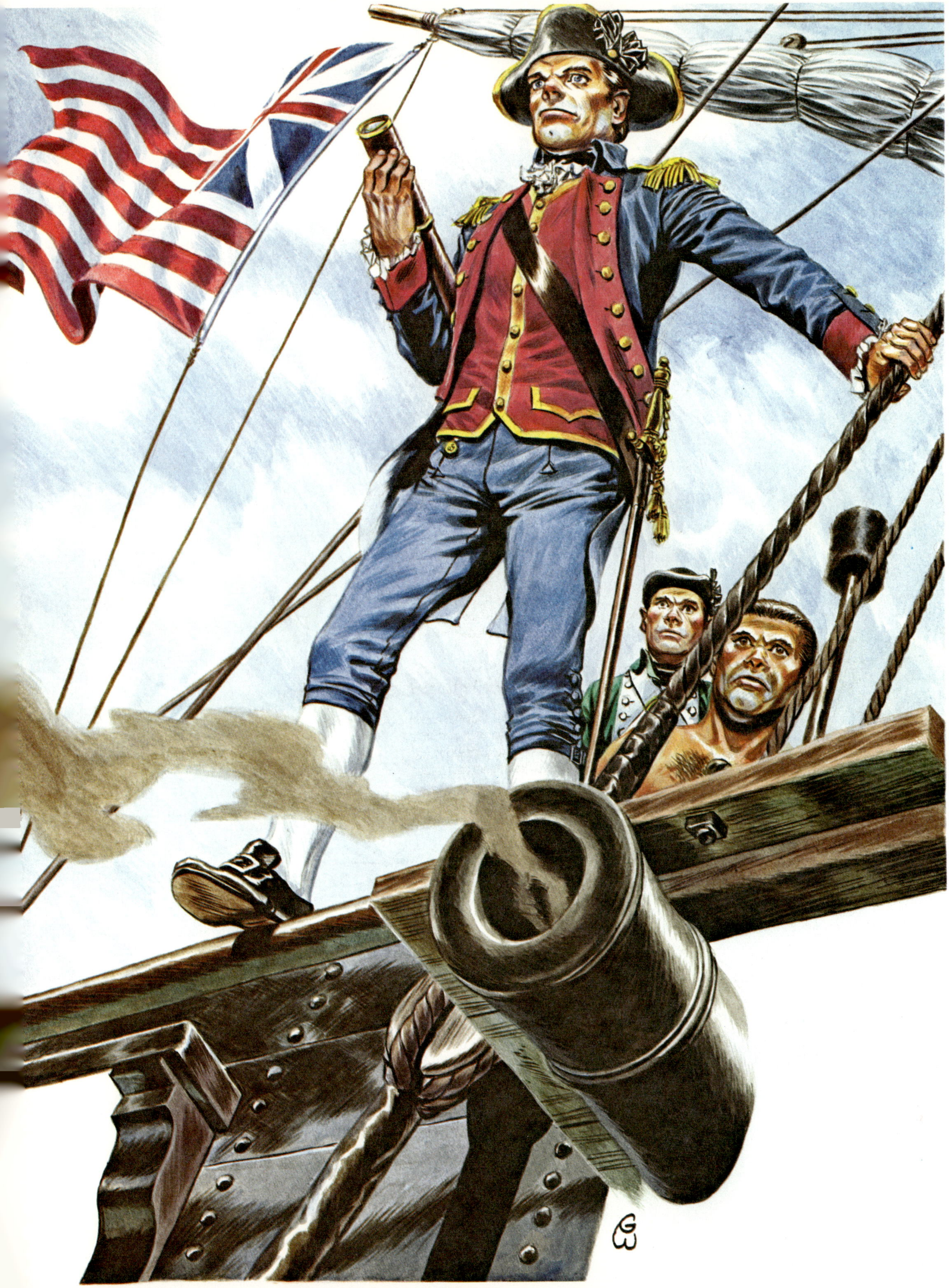

THE TRADESMAN

In hastily formed revolutionary military forces there is no greater need than that for able officers. Any individual among the chaotic mob of belligerent civilians milling about on the outskirts of British-held Boston who displayed any martial aptitude at all would have had difficulty avoiding rapid promotions.

☆☆

A sterling example of the instant commander was Lt. Colonel William Barton, Rhode Island Militia. A little over a year earlier, the Providence hatter had been a corporal in his city's volunteer guard when it marched on Boston. He'd shown a knack for soldiering and eager senior officers had quickly marked his talent. Now, back in his home state, he was second in command of the small American fort at Tiverton, keeping watch on the British garrison in Newport.

It had come as a humiliating shock to the new Yankee officer to learn that an American officer he admired greatly, Major General Charles Lee, an Englishman serving (at least nominally) as General Washington's deputy, had, by sheer chance, been captured by a wandering British patrol. Even worse, the normal pattern of exchanging prisoners of equal rank could not be used to get him back. The Americans lacked a British major general to make a trade.

Barton was an aggressive man. As the merchant hatter he had been, and presumably would be again, he was practiced in the art of dickering. Since the Americans lacked the tradable commodity to buy back their merchandise, it would be necessary to acquire one British major general for swapping purposes.

The supply of available British major generals was small, but adequate. The handiest was the commander of the Royalist garrison occupying Newport. A disgruntled British deserter had been a mine of pertinent information. The English general did not relish the Newport summers. He'd decided he preferred the bracing inland climate enjoyed at the home of a Quaker named John Overing, some four and a half miles from Newport. There are very few inhospitable hosts when a self-invited guest has the support of several thousand bayonets. The British commander did not have a high opinion of the menace presented by the American fort and its garrison. He regarded a squad of eight men and a corporal as a suitable guard detail. The only other British troops nearby were some dragoons who acted as couriers and were quartered nearby.

The business opportunity presented by this situation was one to gladden the heart of a hat merchant. Dressed in nondescript civilian clothing, Barton scouted the area and verified the deserter's description of its physical arrangements. The shore stations, with their offshore naval support, offered no difficulties.

Now, with thirty-six assorted volunteers, he'd slipped past the patrolling frigate *Emerald* in five whaleboats with muffled oars. Ashore, the abduction had been ridiculously easy. The sentries had been overcome without a sound. Barton himself, with only a black artilleryman named Sisson, had broken into the general's room. He'd been the only exception to a generally amiable kidnapping. Mostly, the latter was enraged at being bundled off in such an unceremonious manner. He felt quite strongly that a proper surrender entailed the tender of one's sword and a correct exchange of military pleasantries. He'd discovered that it was practically impossible to retain a commanding presence while being hustled into a whaleboat by a grinning black man and clad only in his regimental coat and a nightshirt before a snickering audience of traitorous rascals and a Rebel officer who kept referring to him as "the merchandise."

By the time it was discovered that the garrison commander was missing, the whaleboats were safely away. British Major General Richard Prescott was not a meek man. As a matter of fact, his temper was notorious. He thundered Jovelike disapproval in giving Colonel Barton the benefit of his opinion of such a shabby manner of waging warfare.

It occurred to Barton that Major General Charles Lee was a touchy man himself. He hoped fervently that the deputy commander was never given an accurate description of the individual the colonel had selected as an equal trade.

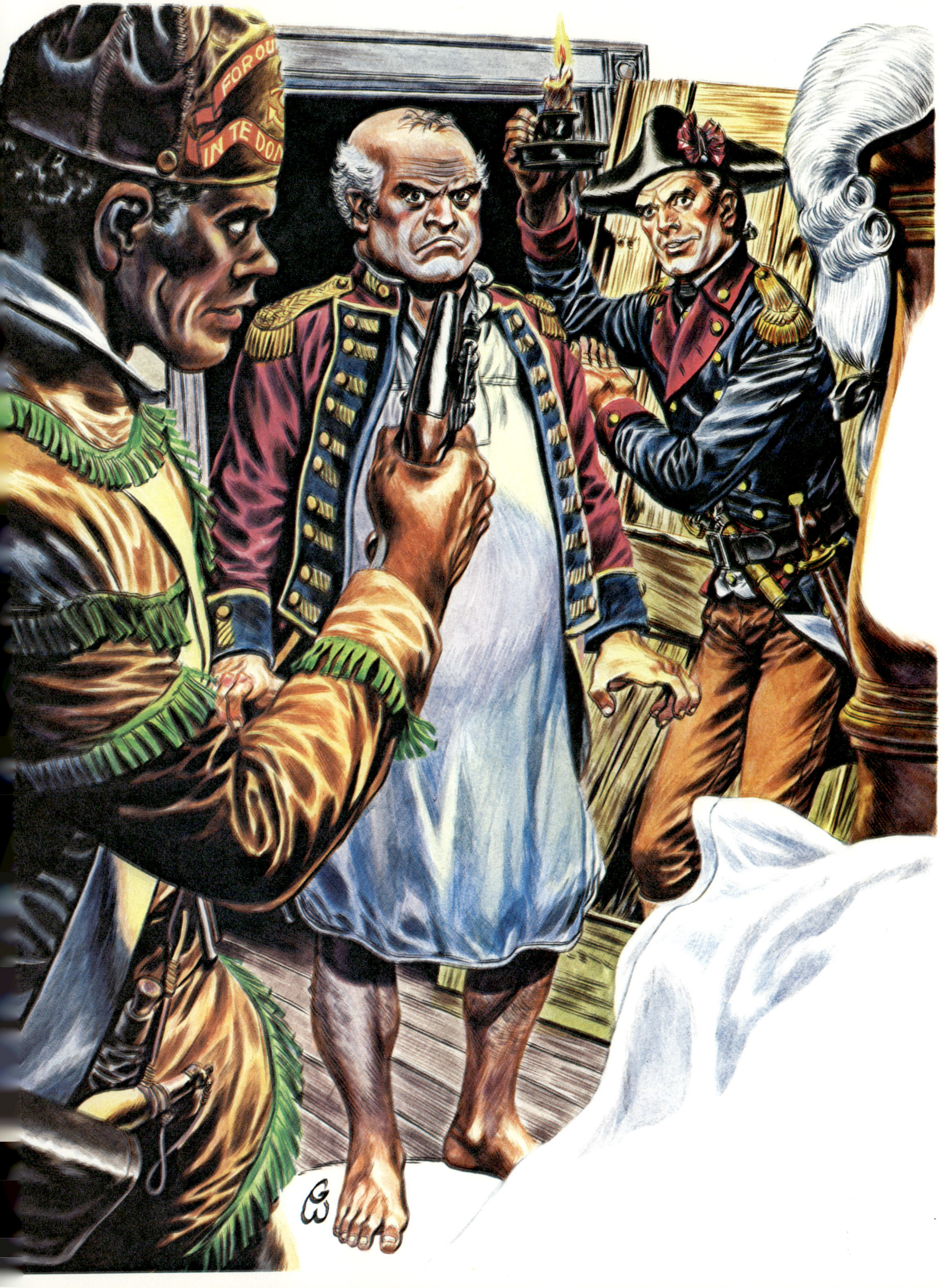

THE PROPAGANDIST

The morale of hard-bitten, professional armies has been known to crack under the sickening shock of repeated defeats. To the ill-prepared civilians of a revolutionary army, emotionally involved and buoyed by illusory enthusiasm, the harsh realities of battles lost can be crushing. Courage begins to wane where memories are crowded with unspeakable images of dead and mangled friends. Now the door is open to mind-numbing weariness and its obscene partner, fear.

To the veteran, the habit of discipline, the countless hours of drill, act as an instinctive brake to emotion. The citizen-soldier's military indoctrination is too shallow for this. If he is to be reached at all, it must be with words. They must be words to touch his heart, to rekindle his spirit, to remind him of high principles, half-forgotten in the chaos of shame-filled routs. A revolution must have an articulate voice for these dark times, one capable of reaching the minds of men at the ends of their ropes. In this respect, the Rebel leaders of the American Revolution were fortunate to have a perpetually angry man, one whose biting, trenchant pamphlets had become the voice of the rebellion.

☆☆

It was a poor, smoking fire. They all were. The wood had been wet and the soldiers who'd foraged for it were too tired to care. Like the others, flickering wanly through the cold rain pounding the muddy fields, it gave off little light and less heat. To the several thousand exhausted men huddled around the fires in sodden, battle-grimed uniforms, the flames were an appropriate accent to the nightmare they'd been living in for as far back as they could remember. Mostly the nightmare had been one of running—fleeing a nameless horror ever at their heels. In it, they'd lost weapons, rations, and above all, self-respect. They were bivouacked on this farmland near Newark, New Jersey, because they could run no farther. Only a fragile thread of almost forgotten common purpose had held them together, plus a grim stubbornness suitable to a pioneering people. It had been their instinct for self-preservation which had dictated that they obey their officers' commands. So, they'd fallen out for the guard details, kicked their bone-weary horses into motion, sweeping the countryside in search of forage. Those not otherwise occupied simply slumped into the mud and stared, hollow-eyed, into the smoldering campfires.

Thomas Paine scarcely noted the inconveniences. The rage at social injustice he lived with was more bitter than usual. The shambling, stumbling retreat across the Jersey meadows, the memory of the ragged columns snaking slowly and painfully through the bogs did not improve his disposition. Now, as he crouched over the drum which served him as a desk and used his cloak to shield paper and writing materials from the rain, he watched, grim-lipped, the gaunt-faced men who moved listlessly between the fires on pointless errands. They had tried so hard, given so much, and now ahead of them there was not even the hope of ultimate success, or even release—least of all victory.

The British had driven this army out of New York and across the Hudson. Now they were gleefully harrying what was left of it after the faint of heart had vanished. Paine, watching them, became aware of words forming soundlessly in his mind—bitter, accusing words, "Sunshine Patriots," "Summer Soldiers!" All the smug, practical men who lay snug in their beds! Unless their consciences could be touched, unless they joined the fight, the Revolution was lost, Thomas Paine dipped his scratchy quill in ink and wrote at the top of the coarse paper, "These are the times that try men's souls. . . ."

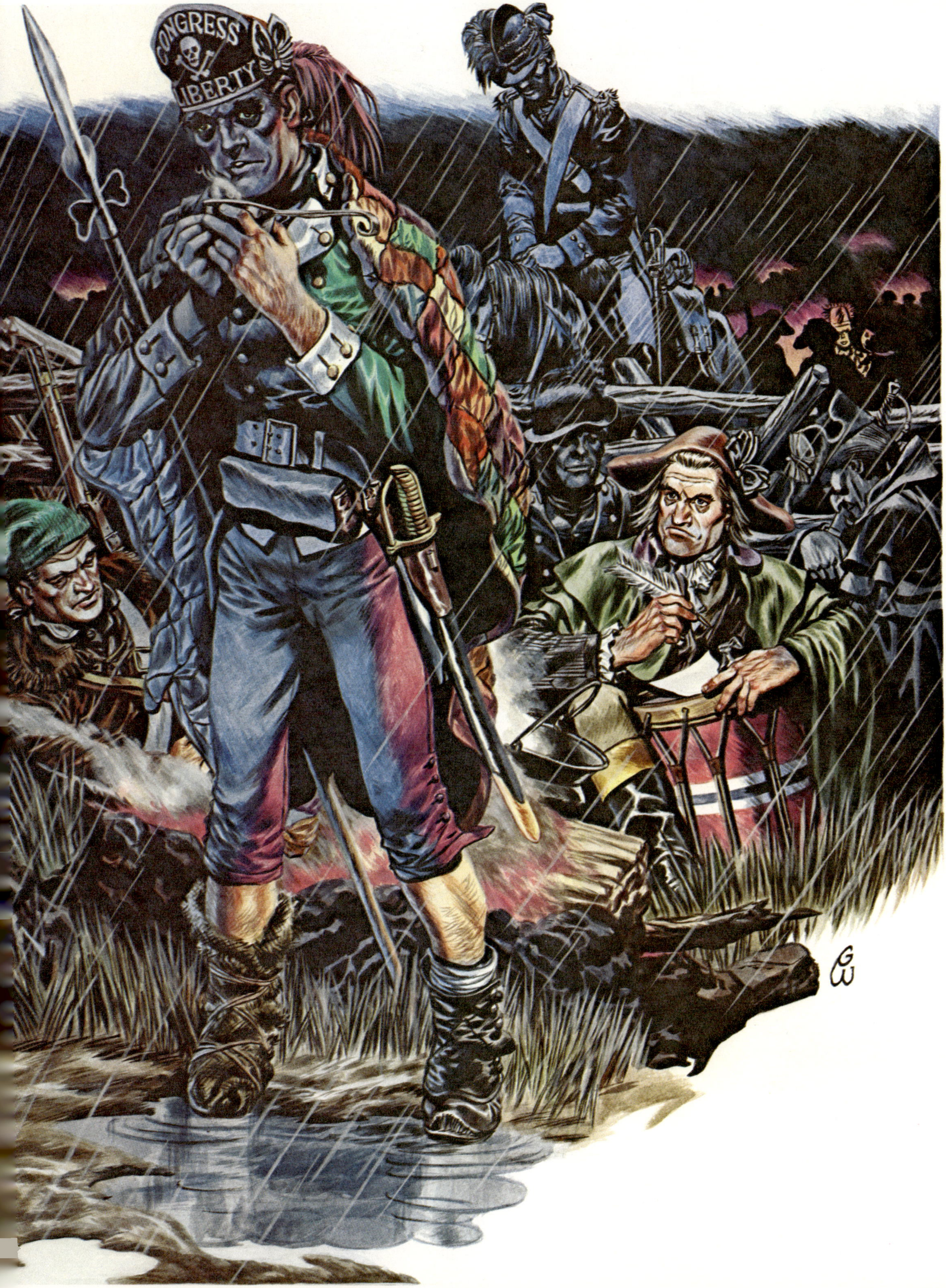
CONGRESS
LIBERTY

THE CATTLE DEALER

It would seem to be a truism that when revolutionary movements reach their lowest ebb, they are at their most dangerous. This would certainly seem to be the case with the infant United States of America in the dreadful winter of Valley Forge. The brutal cold, the seeming hopelessness of the cause, actual hunger, disease, anger at an indifferent Congress, plus the undoubted need to attend to neglected farms and trades, had depleted the ranks of Washington's army. Gone were those to whom loyalty to an unformed, barely recognizable government was less than a life or death matter. Those left, however, were the hard-core Rebels; a fanatically dedicated elite. Like hungry wolves, these reckless men skulked in the shadows, licked their wounds and, with remorseless patience, waited.

☆☆☆

The hearth fire crackled on its bed of glowing coals. The two Continental cavalrymen warmed their hands at it gratefully. It was bitterly cold on this Pennsylvania side of the Delaware, typical of late December. The troopers grinned at each other contentedly. Not only were they enjoying a rare chance to get the everlasting chill out of their bones, but they'd scored a coup which couldn't do them any harm with their superiors.

Their prisoner stood stolidly in the center of the room. His arms were still bound to his sides. His boots were caked with frozen mud and slush. The horse soldiers had forced him to walk between their horses all the rutted miles from the field outside Trenton where they'd taken him. The bastard had put up a devil of a fight, too. Then he'd had the unmitigated gall to claim that he was a simple drover, hunting for stray cattle to sell to the Hessians who had dug in and were holding the town.

He hadn't fooled the dragoons one bit. There was a standing order out to all pickets commanding that one John Honeyman, the notorious Tory and British agent, be picked up on sight. A measure of how important a capture they'd made was the fact that they'd been instructed to bring him directly to this farmhouse, General Washington's personal quarters.

A door opened. At the sight of the big, solidly built man in blue and buff framed in the entrance, the troopers snapped to attention. General George Washington thanked the pair gravely. He commented that it was a deep gratification to him that at this low ebb in their nation's fortunes there were still men who carried on with spirit.

The pair of dragoons had a distinct swagger as they left the room. They carried themselves like men privy to important affairs of state as they informed the sentry outside that the commander in chief wished to question the spy in private. However, if the man made a break for it, he was to be shot down without mercy.

Inside, John Honeyman rubbed his arms to restore circulation. Washington waited patiently, poured two ponies of French brandy, passed one to the prisoner. Honeyman's voice had a rich, Scottish burr. "Their commander is Colonel Rall, the same Hessian who was at Fort Washington's taking. He has not a high opinion of your troops, sir. He's made no preparations to move at all. Instead, the Germans are squeezing the countryside for provender. They're planning a party for Christman Eve. They've enough rum to float every flatboat on the Delaware." The hulking civilian paused. He did not give an opinion lightly. "You can take Trenton, if you want it, sir."

Washington's face showed a hint of a rare smile. "Thank you, John. Your escape will be arranged in the usual manner. Good luck and good night." The commander in chief and his double agent downed their brandies.

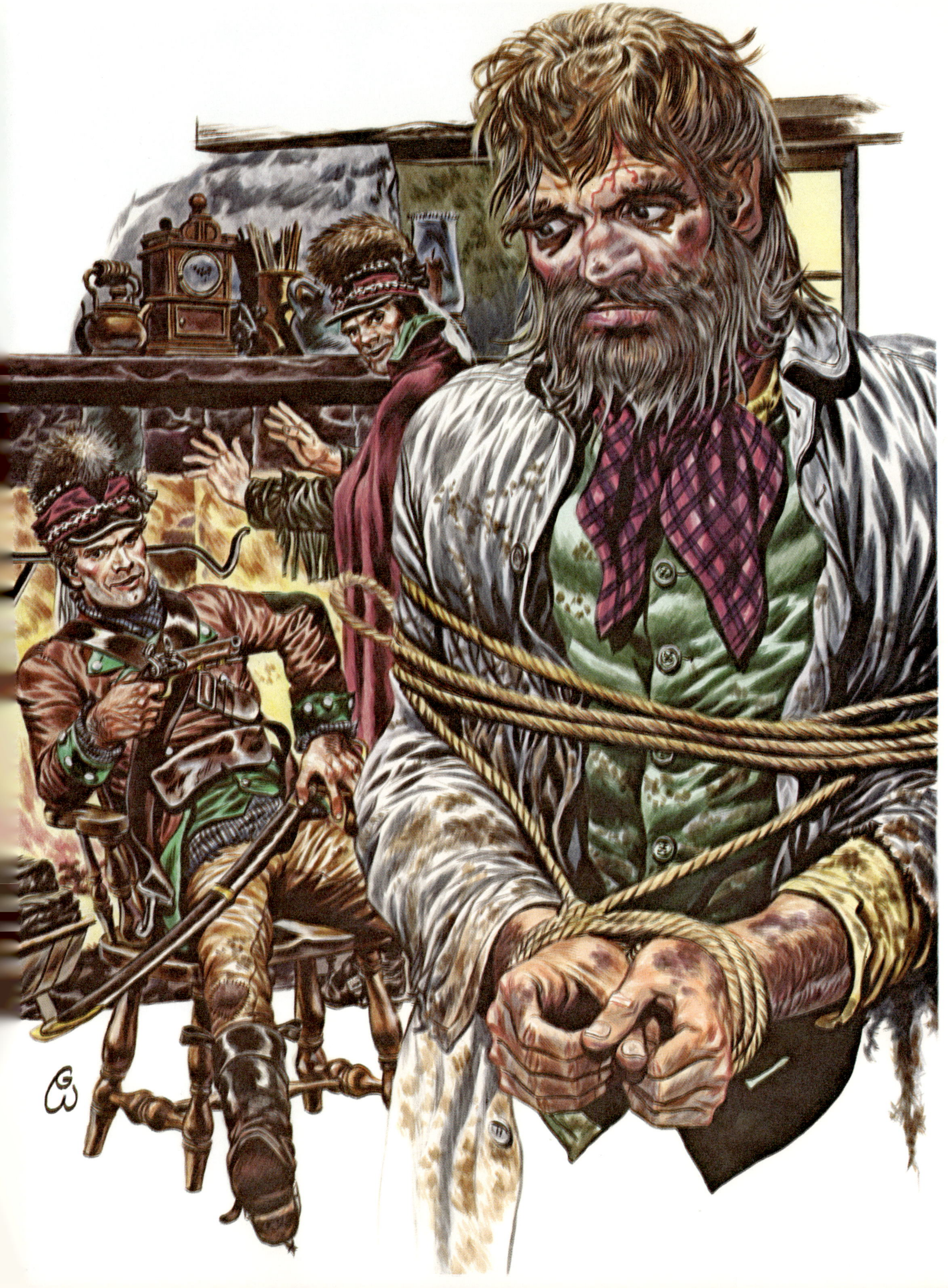

THE FISHERMEN

In a revolutionary army still too primitive to have established its formal branches of service with their own organization, training, and combat mission, it is still common for units, especially those composed of men with a common background and equipped with a similar civilian skill, to evolve naturally into elite troops, uniquely fitted for certain types of battle operations.

Among the raw troops Washington found milling about forlornly behind their entrenchments outside Boston, there was no scarcity of potential specialists. Of no group was this more true than the ragtag militia from the fishing ports along the Massachusetts coast. Deep-sea fishermen by trade, they were skilled small boat sailors, trained by the hazards of dory fishing for cod in the fogs and blows of the Grand Banks.

☆☆

The soldier in the bow thrust his boat hook into the piled up mass of dirty ice with a heave of his shoulders, and cursed fluently. For an instant, the sixty-foot Durham flatboat seemed to stand motionless in the wet, black slick between the floes. Then, imperceptibly, the bow swung clear. At the tiller in the stern, Colonel John Glover of the Marblehead Regiment could scarcely see the forward section of the boat through the swirling ribbons of snow, but the craft's angle of movement told him what was happening. For a little man he had a stentorian voice, well exercised from the quarterdeck of his trading schooner, *Hannah*. "Ahoy the bow! Can you see the shore?" The bow lookout, busy fending off another massive ice structure, yelled something incoherent over his shoulder. A free translation would have informed the amphibious regimental commander that his lookout had serious reservations about the likelihood of there being any dry land—short of China—in their wet, black hell. The general tenor of this observation was recognizable to the group of shivering, miserable artillerymen huddled against their guns in a futile effort to keep the cutting wind from finding the rents in their threadbare uniforms. It did little to improve their morale. The Marbleheaders at the sweeps were too weary after too many crossings to do more than numbly dig their oar blades into the icy water and pull. If it had occurred to anyone aboard the barge, all would have agreed that they must have spent more festive Christmas eves sometime in the barely remembered past.

Glover rasped an order and the rowers slumped over their sweeps. The boat drifted. The seamen-turned-soldiers listened intently. Since orders from Washington's command post forbade lights which could be spotted by some random British patrol, sound alone could be used to identify their bearing. There was sound. The Delaware River was filled with it. The keening of the wind, the rumble and crunching of moving ice. Then, faintly, came a voice. "Glover, where the hell are you? Where are my guns?"

The amphibious commander grinned. He recognized the voice of General Henry Knox, Chief of Artillery. The Marblehead sailors knew that he was on the Trenton side of the river.

A few moments later, the big flatboat crunched through the rim of ice at the shore and a mass of ragged troops came swarming over the side to offload the cannon. All around them in the dark there was the quiet rustle of stealthily moving masses of men. As the units formed up for the surprise attack on the Hessians in Trenton, the Marblehead fishermen stumbled stiffly ashore. It had been a backbreaking job to transport Washington's main force across the river under the weather conditions. They were groggy with fatigue, impelled only by the promise of rest for aching bodies. Then they listened as Glover's voice came out of the darkness. Incredulously, they deciphered his orders. "Marblehead, sling your gear. Sergeants, make sure your men's weapons are in order and that they have full cartouche boxes. We're going in with the initial assault."

Prodded by their noncoms, the men numbly fell in. As their column moved out into the snow and darkness, a plaintive voice seemed to sum up the situation. "And to think that I could've been drawin' bosun's shares if I'd gone privateerin'."

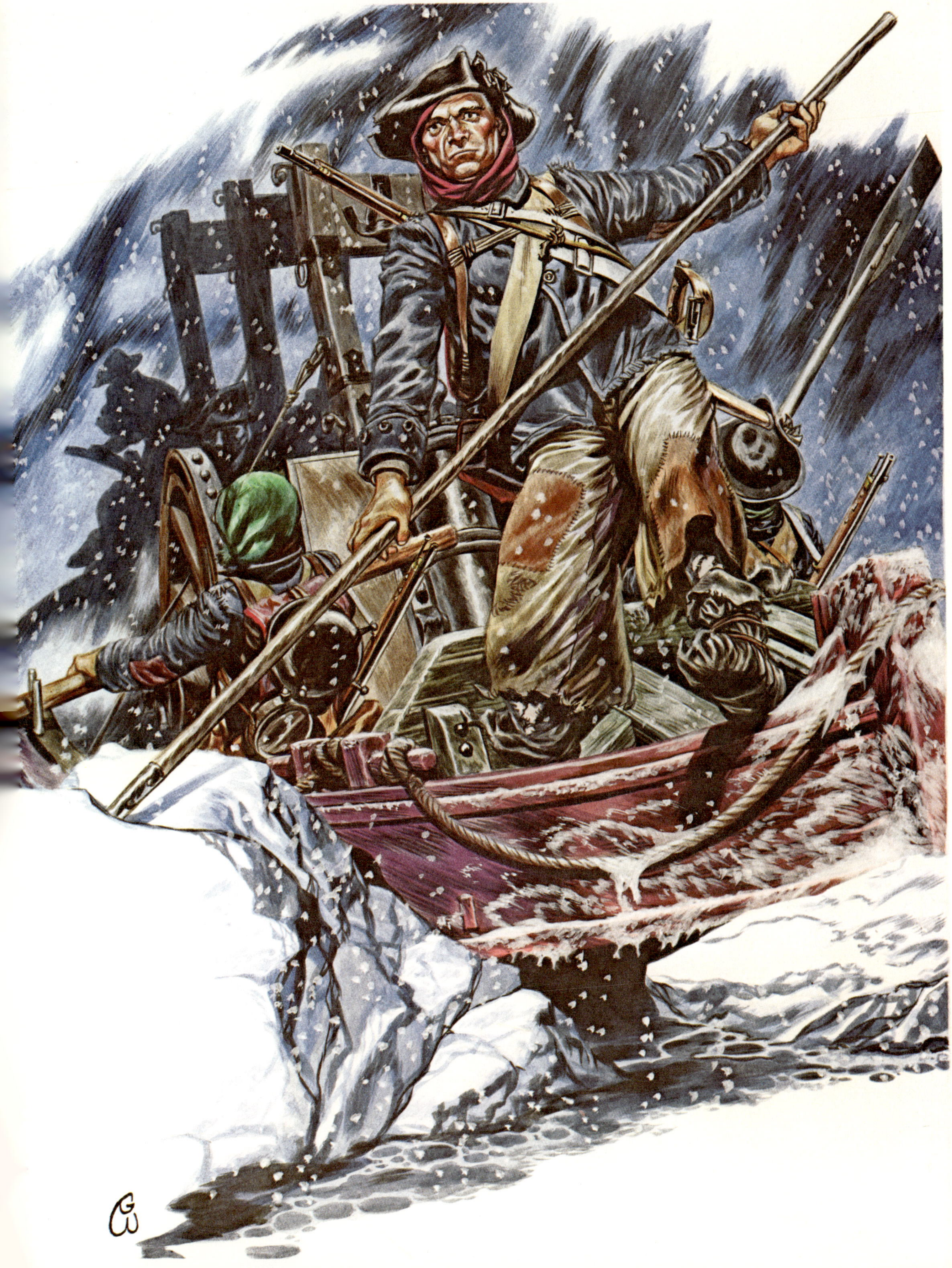

THE PURCHASING AGENT

As it becomes obvious to the watching chancellories of interested nations that a provincial insurrection has progressed from an indignant demand for reforms to a goal of national freedom, the statesmen begin to consider how this can be used to further their own national interests. The temptation to influence the rebellion's outcome accordingly is one no alert foreign minister can resist.

The more sophisticated revolutionary leaders will be aware of this situation and prepared in turn to exploit it for their own national advantage. The infant United States had made its appearance at a time singularly appropriate for such political gamesmanship.

Great Britain and France, rivals for the role of superpower, had fought to a massive showdown only a few years before. The French loss had cost them Canada and a clutch of lesser colonies, as well as domination of Europe. The American Revolution offered them an opportunity to repay the English for their humiliation and perhaps repair their political fortunes as well. The cost and risk involved in clandestine shipment of munitions to North America would be insignificant in view of the potential benefits. The Secret Committee of the American Congress was aware of the opportunity present and they had on the scene a team of agents headed by one of the ablest diplomats of the age, Benjamin Franklin.

☆☆

There was a chill drizzle mixed with fog over the quays. Occasionally the swirling wet lifted, revealing the bay in fleeting patches of steel gray. The French longshoremen, sweating cargo aboard the *Amphitrite* and the *Murcure*, were bawling jovial obscenities at each other. The handsomely dressed American wrapped his cloak about him tighter. Franklin, his superior, had given him responsibility for the smooth transport of this shipment, and Silas Deane was pleased with the way it was going. More carts, pulled by giant Percherons, rumbled over the cobblestones and halted alongside the ships. With block and tackle rigged from the ships' yards, the dockers lifted the canvas-wrapped cylindrical objects from the wagons and dropped them into the vessels' open cargo hatches. Deane glanced around at stray spectators. He was quite sure that Lord Stormont had his British agents somewhere about. The canvas camouflage wouldn't fool them about the cannon, but he hoped that they were impressed that he was observing the formalities of secret warfare. He also knew that such niceties wouldn't stop Stormont from pretending surprised indignation as he protested forcefully to Monsieur le Comte de Vergennes, the French Minister. The French assistance to the American war effort was becoming more open each day. As the aid became more open, the risk of war with Great Britain became greater. Deane knew that both Franklin and Vergennes found this a not unattractive prospect.

A step sounded behind him. The American agent relaxed as he recognized the elegant, mustached Frenchman. Pierre Augustin Caron de Beaumarchais bowed cordially and smilingly commented that the firm of Hortalez et Cie seemed to be doing a thriving export business.

Both men smiled. It seemed improbable that the British Secret Service wouldn't know that Hortalez and Company was a front for the Bourbon kings of France and Spain. Neither gentleman was a devout believer in democracy, but it suited their foreign policy to harass England, the ancient enemy.

The British probably knew also that Beaumarchais—gambler, playwright and bon vivant—was Hortalez et Cie, and the French ministry's best secret agent. Nominally, he owned the ships being loaded as well as others at different French ports. Despite British delaying efforts, the ships were to sail, their cargoes of 12,000 stands of arms, 60 cannon, stores of blankets, and gunpowder, all bound for Portsmouth, Maine.

Both agents knew that the British Secret Service had made more than the usual frantic efforts to keep this cargo of war materiel from leaving. They didn't know that the British failure meant that the munitions would reach the Continental Army at a place called Saratoga in time to welcome a British general known to his friends as "Gentleman Johnnie" Burgoyne.

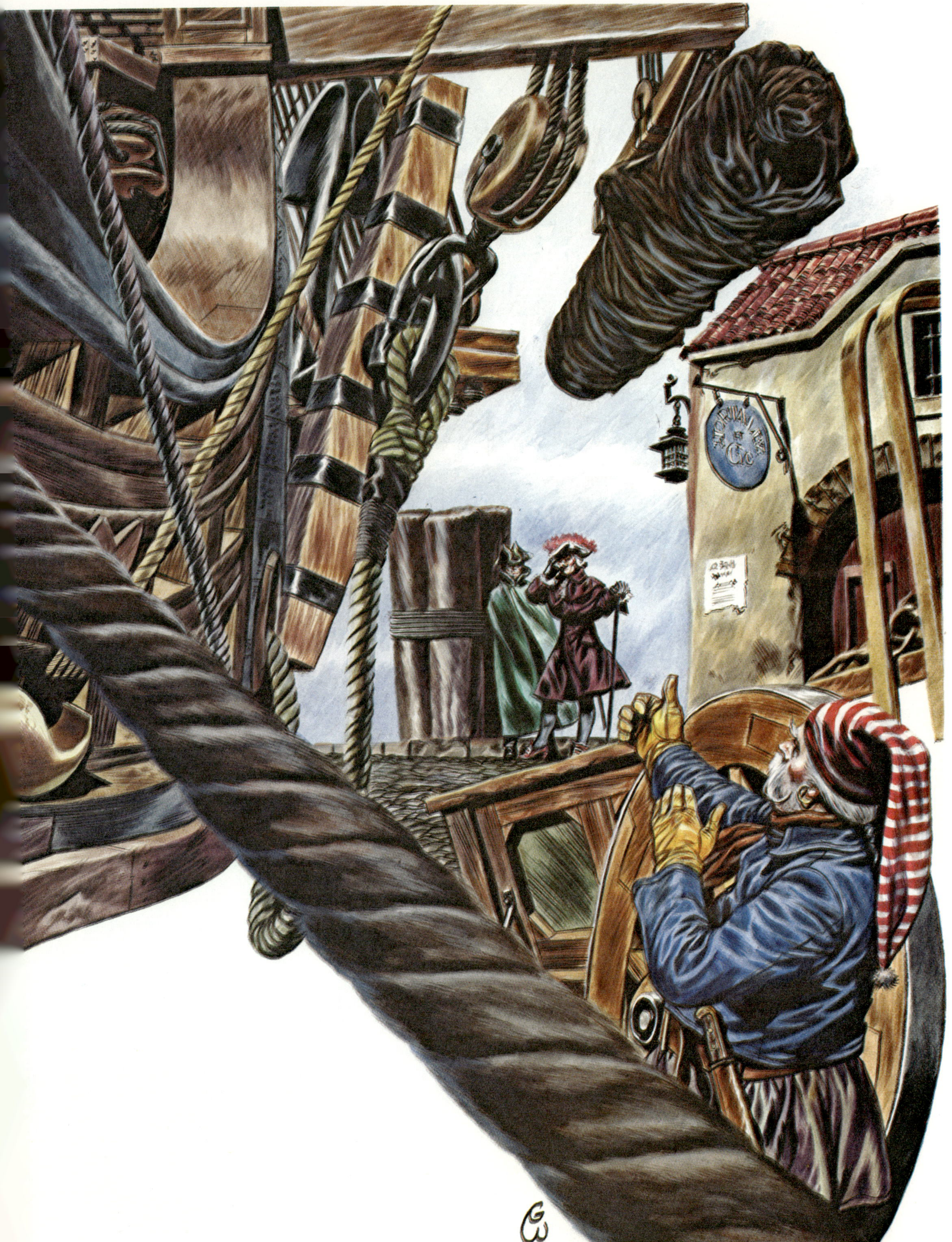

THE BESIEGED

It is the classical pattern of developing revolutions that the parent government eventually will realize that the use of reasonable force will not be enough to bring its insurgents to heel. Inevitably there will be a governmental faction who sees a solution in an extension of the force applied; violence carried beyond the recognized standards of brutality permitted in war. In such a solution, the denial of the rights and customs of war, the use of massacre, summary execution and terror against the exposed civilian population are made to seem acceptable.

Among the men entrusted with the mission of breaking the armed rebellion in the British colonies of North America there were those who favored this tactic, regarded it as unpleasant, but a necessary evil when dealing with traitors to their cherished institution, the monarchy. Unfortunately, they had at their disposal two groups ready and able to carry out a campaign of calculated terrorism; thousands of Tories bitter at those fellow citizens who'd upset their ordered world, and the Iroquois, savage warriors with no concept of mercy, whose chieftains had been induced to become willing pawns of the British military.

☆☆☆

There could have been no more lonely place in the world than Fort Stanwix, at the western end of the Mohawk Valley, a fact of which its garrison was acutely aware. They were York State Militiamen, tough local farmers and under no illusion as to what to expect of the overwhelming force of Iroquois and Tories dug in outside their walls. The nearby presence of 800 British artillery and engineers made the odds against their survival even more astronomical. This combined force, three times their own strength, was commanded by an ambitious English officer, Lieutenant Colonel Barry St. Leger, of his Majesty's Thirty-fourth Foot.

That gentleman had already made his demands known. A British Major Ancrum, under a flag of truce, had been brutally frank. Either Fort Stanwix surrendered at once, or Colonel St. Leger would turn loose his Indians on every man, woman, and child in the entire hundred-mile length of the Mohawk Valley.

The garrison was completely cut off. Their last news had been that their own General Herkimer's militia column had been decimated by Iroquois in a bloody ambush at Oriskany. To their own knowledge, there seemed to be no help in sight. It was even possible their plight was unknown.

Still, they'd sent the envoy packing. Later, an arrow with a document wrapped around its shaft had arched over the wall. It was a copy of a proclamation by the Iroquois's Tory officers, permitting them to massacre all Rebel families in the valley unless the fort surrendered at once.

The American garrison was made up of hard, practical men. They knew the odds. The Iroquois would not find their frontier-wise families submissively helpless. The Yankee troops also knew that their own chances of holding out were minimal, but they knew their antagonists. Surrender would mean mass murder anyway. These farmers of the frontier had faced such options before. They chose two of their ablest woodsmen, Ely Pixley and Ely Stiles, as couriers, with orders to slip through the Iroquois lines and reach whatever American force still survived and report their dire extremity. Then they went back to the frustrating business of trying to impede the underground digging which now preoccupied St. Leger's engineers. Their tunnel was within 150 feet of the northwest bastion. It would be simply a matter of time until that underground gallery was stacked with barrels of black powder and Fort Stanwix's defenses breached.

As the couriers sped stealthily, unseen in the dense forest, they could not know that they passed another party, westbound toward the fort. That rising and daringly devious American general, Benedict Arnold, had invented one of those spectacular plots such as the one which would make him infamous later.

His party consisted of a half-mad, part Indian member of the Tory wing of the Schuyler family, escorted by friendly Oneidas. Hon Yost Schuyler was operating under duress. His brother was Arnold's prisoner. The brother's fate depended on how well he carried out Arnold's instructions.

Shortly, a startled St. Leger found that his Indian allies were deserting in droves. They had listened respectfully to the unbalanced Schuyler's warnings of a rumored American relief force. St. Leger's frantic charges of treason resulted only in the Mohawks looting his camp and baggage train.

Soon, the puzzled garrison of Fort Stanwix discovered that their besiegers were in retreat toward Canada. St. Leger's invasion of the Mohawk Valley expired with a whimper.

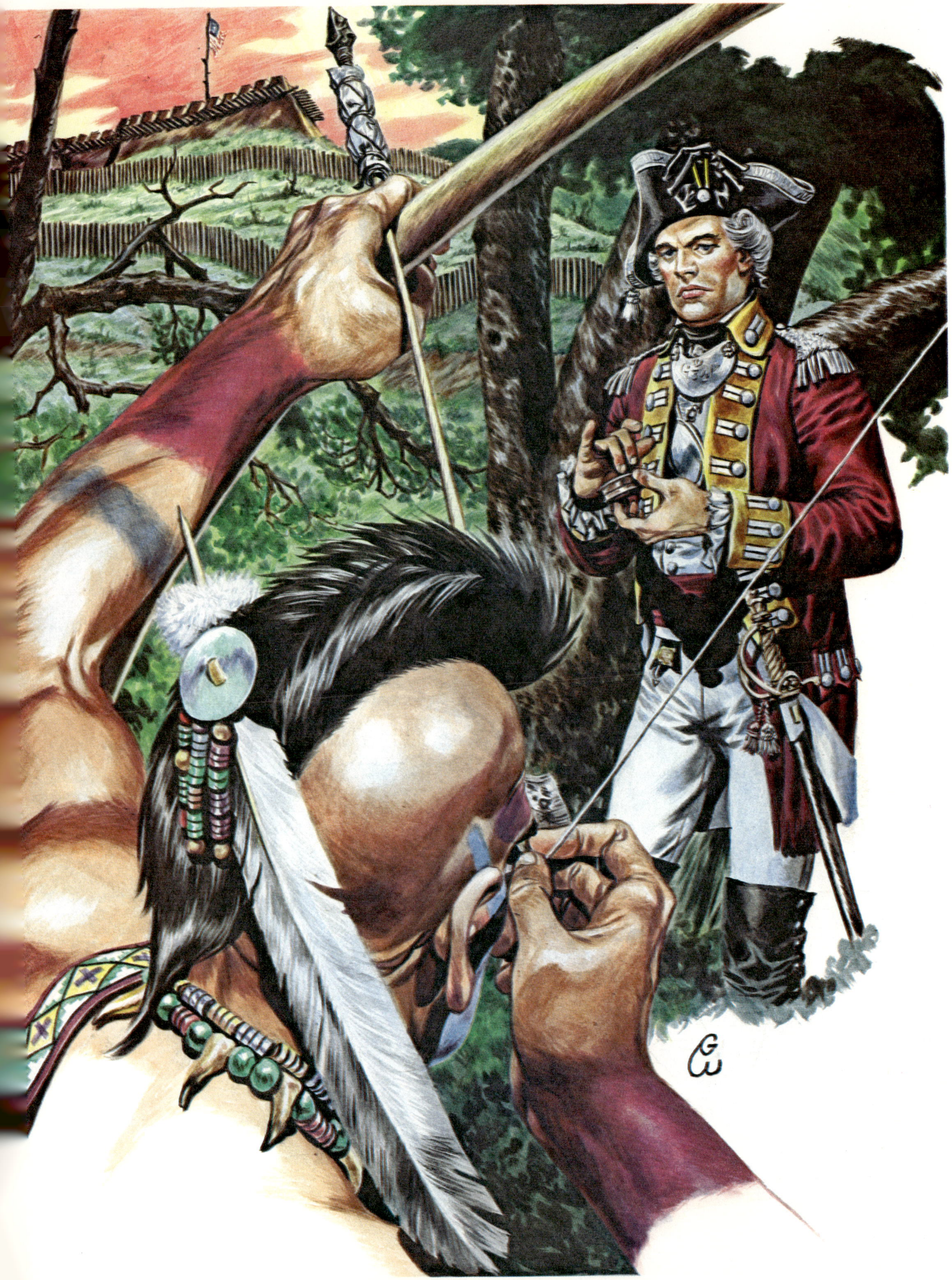

THE STUBBORN MAN

In a revolution, where no orderly leader selection system exists, the able men come to command by a process of natural selection. They stand out among their peers by the very reason that they are nonconformists. If such men are lacking in formidable self-esteem, the dizzying speed with which they often rise soon gives them more than the usual share.

☆☆

The men of the New Hampshire grants were finally becoming irritated at the British. The fighting down in Massachusetts, Connecticut, and New York had seemed a foreign affair. Lumbermen, farmers, and trappers, they were convinced that city people were prone to hysteria. Taking up arms against King George only confirmed their judgment. Also, the British shipbuilders were their prime market for the great trees blanketing their mountains. Then, too, they had a personal war which had been entertaining them for years. This one had evolved around the preposterous claim of the New York Dutch to be overlords of their misty hills. It had seldom heated up beyond the occasional running off of a York sheriff who'd had the bad taste to question their land deeds.

True, some of the boys had gotten in on the king-baiting down around Boston, but the flatland people hadn't been very appreciative—for instance, the way they'd treated John Stark. He'd fought at Bunker Hill, gone with Montgomery and Arnold into the bitter winter, fighting for Quebec. After Trenton and Princeton, they'd made him a colonel, but when Congress had created a roster of new generals, John Stark's name hadn't been on the lists. Thoroughly annoyed, he returned home!

He'd have stayed there, too, if that new British commander, Burgoyne, hadn't started pushing down Lake Champlain. When he took Ticonderoga it had become a personal matter. Their own Green Mountain Boys had overrun that old French fort in the first place.

Burgoyne's activities had made it seem simple prudence to store a suitable supply of war goods at Bennington where it would be handy if needed. John Stark was the natural man to be in charge. He agreed, but not until the General Court of New Hampshire had promised that neither Congress nor the Continental Army would have any authority over him. His name was enough to raise a brigade of fifteen hundred men.

As was to be expected, New York's General Schuyler had sent him orders. The camp at Bennington was full of hilarious rumors of the scandalous refusal Colonel Stark had sent him.

Now Colonel John Stark stood on a point of rock overlooking the Walloomsac River and stared, tight-lipped, at the figures dimly seen through the rain, digging in across the river. It hadn't been Johnnie Burgoyne's most intelligent move. Sending Colonel Baum, a Hessian cavalryman (with a polyglot force of Tories, Indians, and alleged British marksmen attached to his main force of newly arrived mounted Brunswicker dragoons), to search and destroy the arsenal at Bennington was a mistake. The column was not an ideal unit to deal with sharpshooting, country-wise woodsmen.

The Hessian colonel had thrown up a log citadel and prepared to give battle, confident that, with von Breymann, another German officer, coming up in support with several hundred Hessian grenadiers, these rustics were to be given a lesson in the horrors of war.

It was a while later, after an American grenade had exploded his last wagonload of ammunition, and with the New Hampshire attacks coming closer and closer, that Colonel Baum gave an order and his dismounted dragoons dropped their empty carbines and drew their long swords. It was a futile gesture, emphasized by Baum's being dropped by a musket shot. He died as his men surrendered.

Von Breymann fared little better. By nightfall, the survivors of his grenadier companies were in frantic, disordered retreat. The troops that had stood, rocklike, under cannon fire on the battlefields of Europe, ran terror-stricken, pounding down muddy roads in the dark. Finally Stark called off the pursuit.

The Congress, which had just sent a resolution to New Hampshire rebuking Colonel Stark for failing to obey General Schuyler's orders, had to hastily follow it with a commission as brigadier general in the Continental Army, addressed to a stubborn mountain farmer.

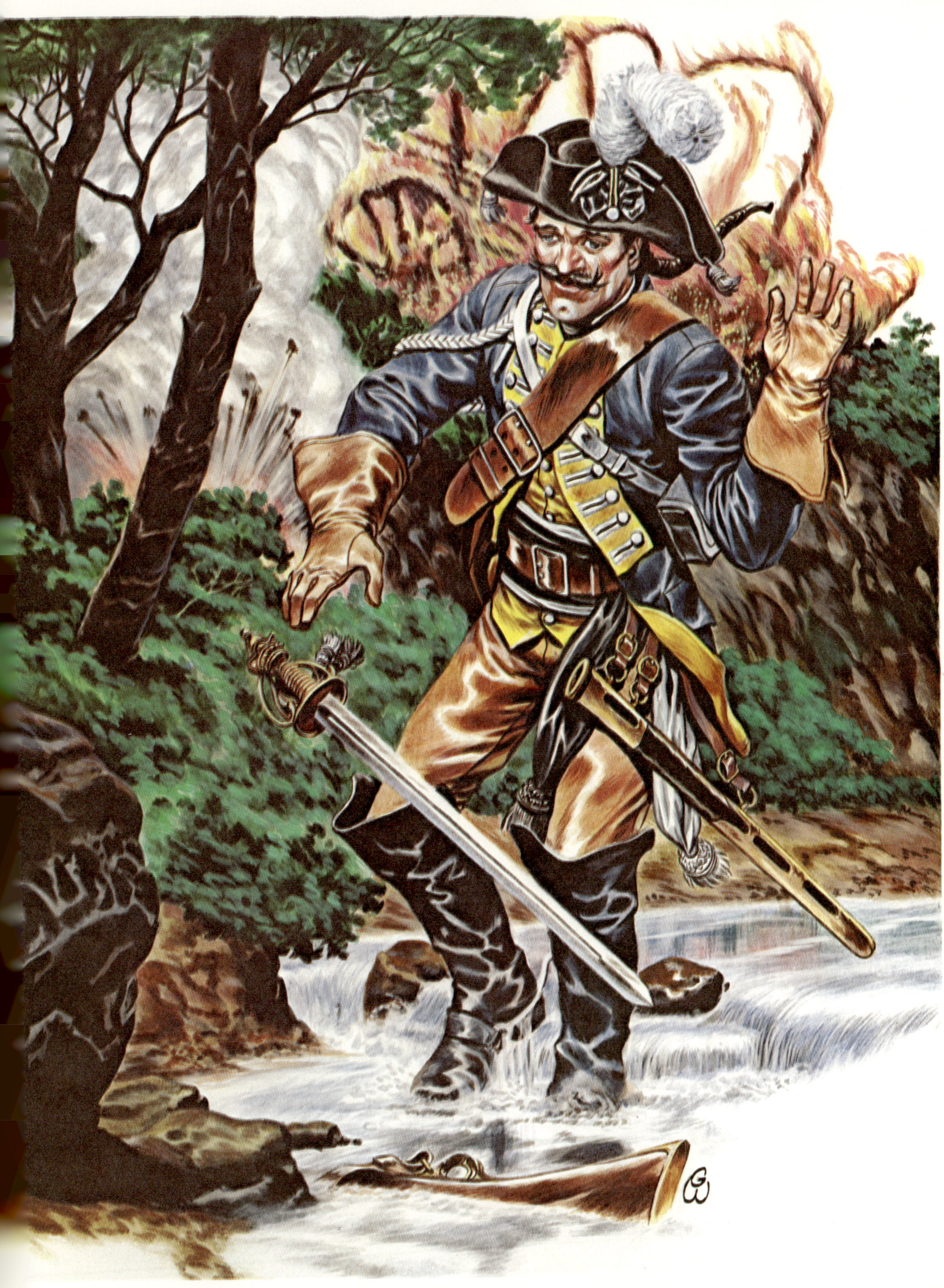

THE LEGENDARY HERO

Perhaps it is a form of revolt against the obscene brutality of combat as the soldier knows it, but he has always cherished a streak of romanticism. Since the first armed rabbles clashed in long-forgotten causes, the man in the ranks has had his own heroes: paladins not by rank or civilian reputation, but great warriors by the common soldier's own standard of excellence. Often enough, these champions have been half-myths, their exploits the deeds of many brave men. Occasionally, there has been an individual, one whose courage and steadfastness have earned him the awed respect of his peers, whose existence is a matter of historical record.

The 10th Virginia Line of the Continental Army was fortunate enough to have such a soldier in its ranks. In addition, as if his frequent assaults upon the soldiery of George III weren't enough, there was a mystery surrounding his background as well. Most citizens of Buckingham County knew how he'd been put ashore as a small boy from an unidentified ship, speaking only what was thought to be French and Portuguese and that he'd been taken in and raised by Judge Winston. The circumstances had convinced the ladies of the county that he was the product of some European political scandal and was surely of royal blood.

☆☆☆

Sir William Howe had found the use of the flanking maneuver extremely effective against General Washington's Army at Long Island, Manhattan, and White Plains. Now he was hopeful that it would give him Philadelphia and New Jersey as promptly as it had New York.

The Americans had obliged Howe by electing to make a stand along a stream called Brandywine Creek. With the confidence born of successful experience, the British commander sent a feinting force against the Rebels at a spot called "Chadd's Ford," while his main division swung upstream to hit the Yankees' right flank.

The tactic had been carried out flawlessly. As an added guarantee of success was the item that the American right flank was commanded by General John Sullivan, whose bad luck was proverbial in both camps.

Surprisingly, Sullivan's corps had refused to disintegrate in the routine manner. Faced by overwhelming force, they'd retreated slowly, stubbornly, and in good order. Then, too, Washington had reacted faster than Howe had anticipated. The Virginian quickly pulled General Nathanael Greene and his Old Dominion infantry out of Chadd's Ford and ordered them to support Sullivan. The British found it hard to believe that the 10th Virginia covered four and a half miles in forty-five minutes.

They'd arrived in time to take up a covering position under whose protection Sullivan's mauled columns were able to withdraw. Among those who noted that a gigantic private kept the 10th Virginia as steady as a rock was a newly-arrived French volunteer, the Marquis de Lafayette. He couldn't know that the soldier was a six-foot-six 250-pound adolescent. Peter Francisco was fifteen years old.

The action ended in a draw, though as Howe noted with misgivings, for the first time the Americans had fought a tough, intelligent fight. He suspected the farmers, the traders, and the adventurers were becoming an army instead of a loose grouping of provincial militias.

Having a minor wound dressed at an aid station in a nearby Quaker farmhouse, the Marquis was similarly impressed. General Wayne, a Pennsylvanian, had commanded New Jersey troops. Greene, from Rhode Island, saved Sullivan's wing with Virginians. Evidently, these colonials were evolving rapidly into a new continental type. What would these new Americans be like?

Then the French noble noted the same huge young soldier from the 10th Virginia Line being treated nearby. He noted Peter Francisco's swarthy, Iberian face and his bulk. Obviously, these Americans would be a various people, indeed!

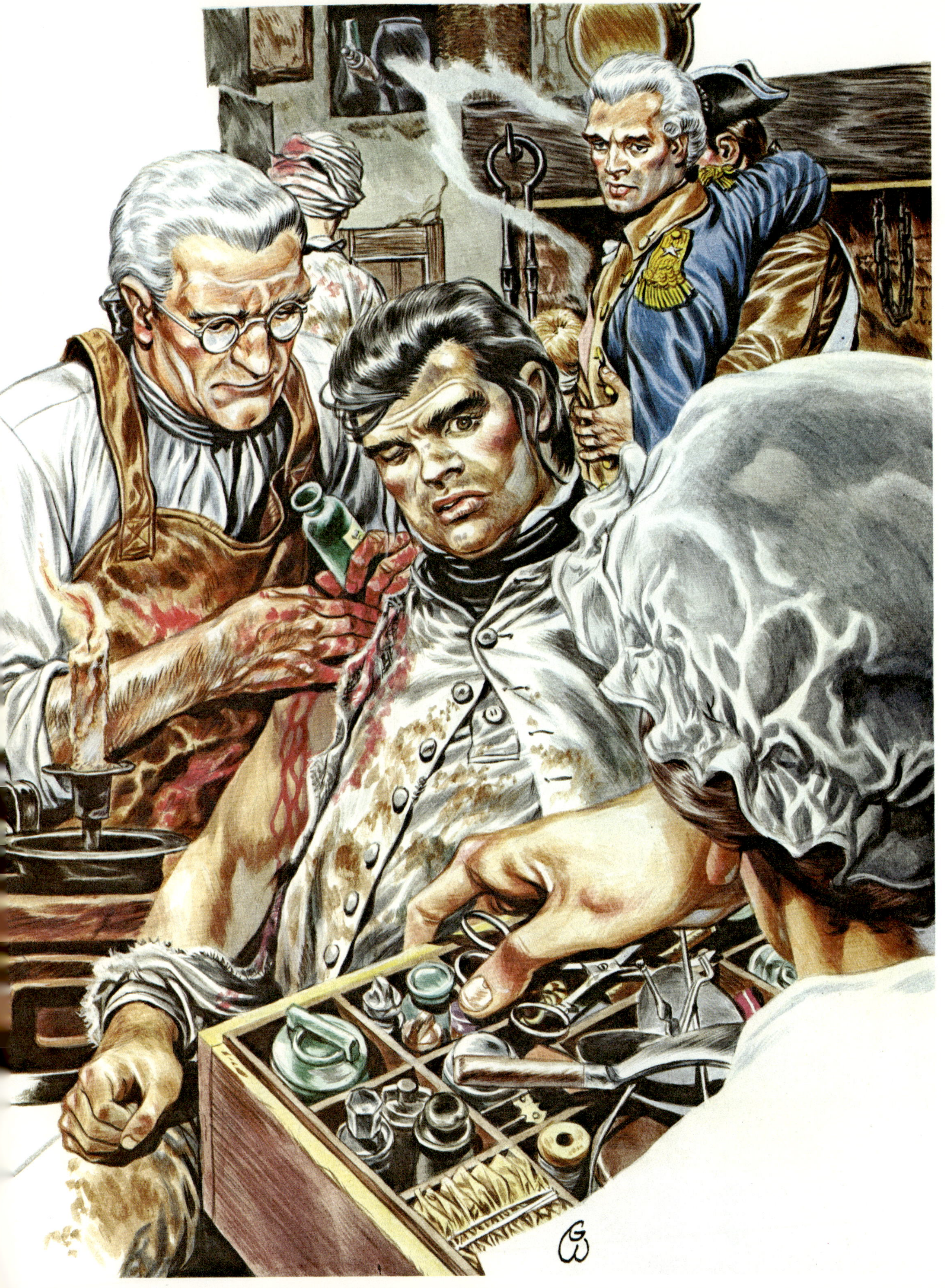

THE LOYAL OPPOSITION

When a revolutionary movement finds itself forced, step by step, to the ultimate decision; to sever its connection with its political parent, its individual citizens will have been pushed to that same moment of truth. Since men are individuals, their judgments colored by different attitudes, they will not all exercise their options in the same way. The factionalism so brought about between members of a closely knit society must be deep and bitter.

The schism which developed between Americans of the rebelling British colonies was no exception. The tradition of loyalty to the British Crown, tempered by the political and religious turmoil of England's past, was a strong one. Great numbers of colonials, angry themselves at London's measures, were still shocked and horrified when dissent became armed rebellion. Just as the Rebels grimly filled the ranks of the Continental regiments, the Loyalists, whom history was to call "Tories," enlisted in the hastily formed "British Royal Provincial Regiments." The hatred between these opposing formations was to be personal and ferocious.

☆☆☆

Despite the best efforts of the Dutch farmers of the York State Militia, Fort Montgomery, key bastion of the Rebel complex designed to deny the Hudson River to the British forces of General Sir Henry Clinton, was dying. The fort's garrison couldn't know it, but they were to die because of a master plan formulated in distant London. The plan called for General Clinton's army to force the Hudson and to link up at Albany with General Burgoyne, who would strike down from Canada and St. Leger. He would drive east through the Mohawk Valley, thus cutting the rebellious colonies in two.

Sir Henry's attack had begun auspiciously. Pushing north from New York City, he'd tricked the American commander, Israel Putnam, leaving him stranded on the wrong side of the Hudson while he concentrated on the Yankee fortifications on the other. The guns of the British fleet on the river, convoying the troop barges, had alerted the valley farmers. From every point of the lower Hudson, they'd come running to reinforce the tiny garrisons of Continentals and militia holding the river forts. Without uniforms or proper equipment beyond their hunting guns, they'd given battle to Sir Henry's British, Hessian, and Tory regiments.

Again and again, Sir Henry had thrown his veteran British and German infantry against Fort Montgomery. Its defenders, hopelessly outnumbered, had still thrown back the assaults, but each effort had taken its toll. Finally, Clinton had thrown his Tories of the "Loyal American Regiment" in for the kill.

These Royalists, mostly recruited from this same Valley, had known the surviving men of the garrison as friends and neighbors. Now, with blind hatred that gave or asked no quarter, these two were fighting it out with cold steel in the ravished fortification. In such a fight, numbers must count.

The fort commander, Colonel George Clinton, distant cousin of the British commander and governor of New York State, gave an order and in the darkness and confusion, those Americans still on their feet began melting away. The Dutch farmers were executing a classical guerrilla ploy. They reassembled a few miles north of Montgomery.

Sir Henry was a cautious man now. He'd been at Bunker Hill and the river fort had added to his respect for these embattled farmers. After some delay, he resumed his northward push, harassed by militiamen every step of the way. By the time he reached Kingston, New York, he was a thoroughly frustrated man. He gave vent to his displeasure by ordering the town burned. Any improvement in his temper was unnoticeable, once he received two messages there. One from the north simply informed him that he was too late. "Gentleman Johnnie" Burgoyne was surrendering. The other was from General Howe. He and his troops were needed to help defend Philadelphia against Washington's main force.

Sadly, the British expeditionary force boarded their vessels and pointed their bows back toward New York. The grand design was dead.

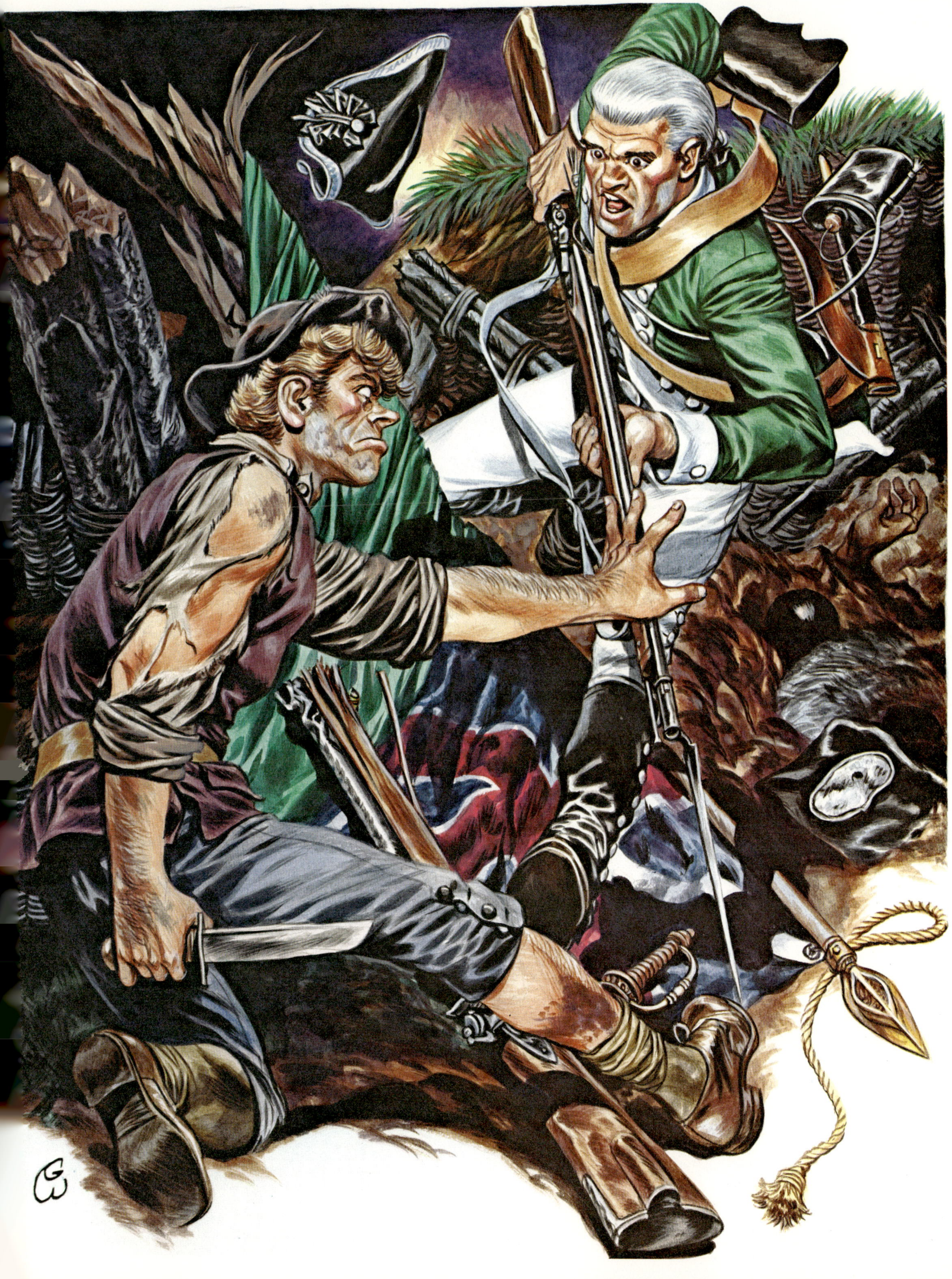

THE TACTICIAN

As a revolutionary army endures and its leaders gain experience, they are less and less impressed by outside experts. Their attitude is apt to be that their hard-won knowledge of the enemy, the terrain, supply problems and above all, the comparative strengths of the opposing troops, is a military skill superior to the formal knowledge of foreigners.

After over two years of hard campaigning, most of it in difficult retreat, the seasoned senior officers of the Continental Army rightly felt that they had learned to fight their enemy and their war. Many, especially those without previous European contact, were suspicious of the abilities of the foreign officers, volunteers, and mercenaries, now arriving in numbers. The newcomers' formal manners, their attention to elaborate military protocol, and standardized maneuvers, all clashed with the Americans' ingrained egalitarianism.

☆☆☆

Daniel Morgan, commanding the Ranger regiment, glanced suspiciously around the tent. Arnold was there, sardonic and secretive. Morgan knew him to be recklessly daring. Also present were Horatio "Granny" Gates, the ex-British major from a nondescript regiment, commanding general of this army more by whim of Congress than anything; Schuyler, too, the aristocratic New Yorker who'd made "Gentleman Johnnie" Burgoyne pay for every foot of his invasion. But the attention of the American commanders was centered on the foreigner with the unpronounceable name and baffling accent.

Morgan had serious doubts that any of these elegant, posturing Europeans should be taken seriously. They might be well and good for organizing parades, but this war in the wilderness was a different matter. Now, this improbable Pole was addressing him, indicating a tangle of lines and symbols drawn on a map. Morgan knew what he was discussing. The map showed the area known as "Bemis Heights" just below the village of Saratoga.

This was where Burgoyne had been brought to bay. His line of retreat had been made impassable, he'd lost 900 Hessians at Bennington. He was without supplies or hope of reinforcement. He had to fight. The Pole had designed the redoubts and entrenchments used by the Americans. Now he was proposing how Morgan should deploy his unit and the frontiersman resented it. He'd been touchy since his elite troops' weakness had been made obvious. Their long rifles took too much time to reload and their tomahawks were useless against British bayonets. They could only snipe and retreat. Morgan's mouth was a grim line. What the hell did this macaroni know about ambush and harassing fire, about cutting off flankers and picking off commanders?

The Pole glanced curiously at the frontiersman. He'd had to deal with independent-minded commanders before. He recognized the type. That made two who would probably ignore his recommendations. The dark general, Arnold, was obviously eager to enhance his already formidable reputation. He shrugged. It was the military engineer's job to prepare for the contest. Its outcome would depend on others.

When combat came, the Pole's preparations proved highly effective. If Gates hadn't been so cautious, Burgoyne's army would have died under the fire from its positions. Even so, Arnold's bold charges and Morgan's deadly sniping made the British surrender inevitable.

It was in the heat of the fight that Morgan recognized how well the foreigner had planned. The desperate charges of the Royal grenadiers, the frantic lunges of the Hessians—both ended in bloody disaster, cut down by enfilading fire from the dug-in Americans. The lines on the map had been a blueprint for an army-devouring trap.

It was when what was left of the scarlet-coated regiments were drifting back toward the village and eventual surrender that Morgan noticed the Pole astride his horse on a rise, watching the retreat with professional detachment. The slim foreigner was startled when the burly American appeared and slapped him resoundingly on the knee. General Daniel Morgan made some jovially obscene comments which the Pole was unable to decipher. However, Colonel Thaddeus Kosciusko, Polish aristocrat and patriot, felt himself flattered at this indication of acceptance by so obviously a genuine democrat.

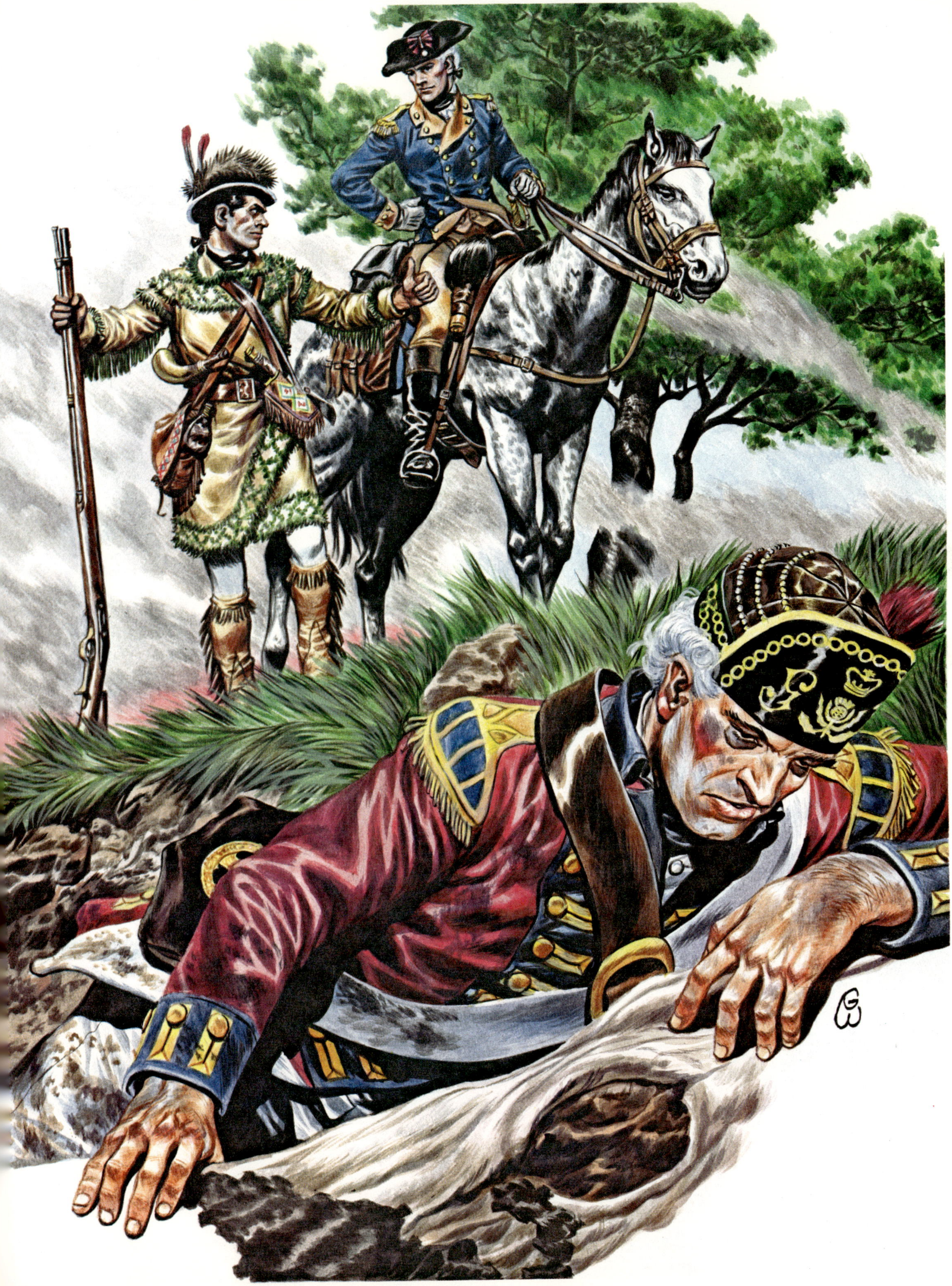

THE INVENTOR

The history of warfare is liberally salted with the introduction of unconventional killing machines. Often, they have been proved upon testing to be spectacularly impractical. Occasionally, one has held the germ of a workable idea, requiring only proper adaptation to become a standard device for the destruction of individuals too benighted to appreciate the superior moral position of the inventor.

Few of these innovators are soldiers. The military man, with more training and experience, more conscious of the penalties of defeat, is more apt to depend on traditional methods of populating the enemy's military cemeteries. Uninhibited by any actual contact with the nightmare realities of a recently contested battlefield, the imaginative civilian is capable of creating lethal machines so grisly that startled enemy commanders are reduced to brooding upon the unfortunate results of allowing amateurs to participate in what had been a gentleman's profession.

☆☆☆

The rivermen handled the strange objects with nervous care. Their hands were cold to begin with, there was an icy wind blowing across the Delaware River at this point, and they had received a graphic description of what would happen if one of the contraptions were to be accidentally detonated. The creators of these odd-looking floats, David Bushnell of Connecticut and his associate, a man named "Carman," gingerly checked each of the twenty machines as it was skidded to the side of the river boat, ready to be launched. This procedure did little to quiet the boatmen's nerves. If this entire affair hadn't been sponsored by the formidable Francis Hopkinson, signer of the Declaration of Independence and chairman of the Continental Navy Board, they'd have resigned immediately after hearing Bushnell describe how the first working model of his "mine" had come close to blowing up the British warship *Cerberus* off Saybrook, Connecticut. The rivermen's trust in Bushnell's stability hadn't been strengthened by reports of his other invention. This mind-boggler was apparently a submersible boat of some sort. It had been called the *Turtle*. Incredibly, it was supposed to be able to navigate under water. It had been tried out in New York Harbor. A Continental sergeant inside it had allegedly maneuvered it to the underside of a moored British frigate. Only the fact that the ship's bottom was copper-sheathed, which prevented the *Turtle*'s boring mechanism from securing the explosive charge, saved the ship.

These "mines" were Bushnell's latest experiment in reducing the effective strength of the Royal Navy. Each consisted of a watertight, sealed container of black powder, buoyed by a pair of empty kegs and to be detonated by a spring-lock device. This would be activated by contact with the hull of a victim. The spark of the flintlock would explode a charge large enough to seriously breach the heaviest-timbered hull.

Now, on this frigid December night, Bushnell was supervising the launching of a flotilla of these contraptions from a point in the Delaware some distance above Philadelphia where an armada of British warships, transports, and small craft lay at anchor among the floating ice. The Americans were to find that their river-clearing operation was poorly executed. The launching point was far above the target fleet and the current was slow. This led to a severe miscalculation of the time required for the mines to reach their destination. Bushnell became uncomfortably aware of this when it became apparent that it would take over a week for the mines to reach the British moorings. Actually, it was on January 5, 1778, that a barge crew spotted a floating mine and hauled it aboard. The resulting explosion alerted every British sea captain in port.

After some confusion, the source of the danger was identified. The British captains wisely decided that it was better to be ridiculous and afloat, rather than dignified and sunk. They opened up with a cannon and small-arms barrage directed against every floating object in the river. This included driftwood, stray pilings, miscellaneous small craft, and each other. The bombardment continued until nightfall.

The citizenry of Philadelphia, crowding the wharfs, watched, with undisguised glee, as the Delaware reverberated to the ragged cannonading of what was to become known as "The Battle of the Kegs." By the time a night wind had whipped away the last shreds of cannon smoke, the wits, songsmiths, and poets of Philadelphia were already hard at their crafts. The theme was hilarity, the sarcasm biting. Everyone enjoyed the occasion immensely—except David Bushnell.

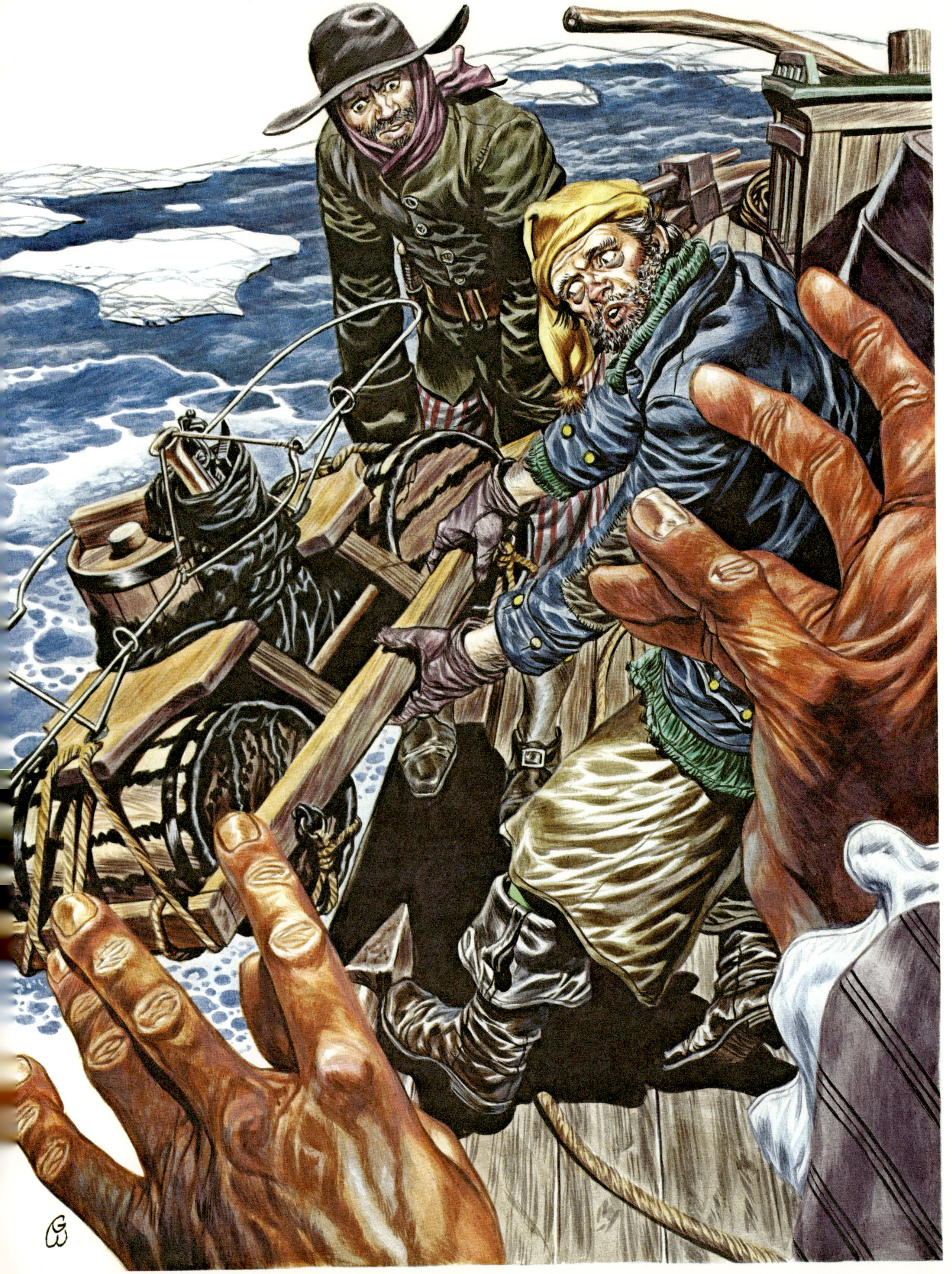

THE TEACHER

In order for a revolution to legitimatize itself, it is necessary for its proponents to take and hold territory—to establish themselves as masters, in fact—of some piece of real estate where they are sovereign. This requires more than the hit-and-run guerrilla raid by now-and-then soldiers. It can be done only by regular troops, able to defend what is already under the flag, and add to it if policy so dictates.

In the 18th century, the infantry was indeed the "Queen of Battles." George Washington, an infantry officer himself, was acutely aware of this. If he had needed any further endorsement of his view, the humiliating failures of the American Army, often with superior firepower, to hold its ground against the savage mass assaults of the British and Hessian ground troops, would provide it. He was aware that his command would average as many brave men to the regiment as the soldiery of any nation. What was needed was training, the everlasting drill which enables a soldier to stand fast, despite the instinctive panic that self-preservation breeds in men. In the American forces, where the officers understood this principle as little as their men, the drillmasters would have to come from elsewhere.

☆☆☆

The men of the battalion had become used to being stared at. The lean, ragged troops who'd survived Valley Forge watched them uneasily as the unit halted, its ranks impeccable. An order rang out and 200 musket butts hit the ground as one. Every man was at rigid attention, eyes straight forward. Not by so much as a wink did any man of the training battalion betray a swagger at the impression it was making on Washington's Continentals.

Two officers began the inspection. The senior was faultlessly uniformed as a major general in the American service. His eyes swept each man, noting, commenting. Colonel Alexander Hamilton, deferentially at his side, translated from the only language the German shared with him: French.

In the cold hell of Valley Forge, a strange change was taking place. The Baron von Steuben had turned up in camp, seeking like many another European mercenary before him, employment at his trade. Many Americans believed that his claim to having been an aide to Frederick the Great was a lie. His assertion that he'd been a lieutenant general was even less probable. However, Benjamin Franklin, who'd recruited him, knew that rank impressed the Congress. Also, both General Washington and Colonel Hamilton did believe that the German could rectify the Continentals' greatest shortcoming—their lack of that rigid discipline which the British infantry possessed in such abundance.

It had been von Steuben's idea to create this elite battalion. Once trained, it would serve as Washington's new personal bodyguard. By rotating promising young officers and noncoms in and out of it, training cadres would be distributed through the Army. In time, the American forces were to become as steady as any in the world.

The inspection finished, the two officers stopped, turned, faced the rigid rows. Hamilton's voice rang out in the crisp early spring air. The Baron wished to have his compliments conveyed. He was pleased with the battalion's appearance. The first company was to be detached to return to their former units as drill instructors. Von Steuben paused, gazed thoughtfully at the ground. As Inspector General, he must decide when they were ready for the responsibility they would carry.

He knew that, like the British officer corps, the Americans had been accustomed to leaving the drilling of troops to corporals and sergeants. The units they were about to command would be their personal responsibility. It would be their duty to make sure that every man was treated fairly. More than that, they were to assure themselves that every man's problems became theirs. They would be held accountable for every man under their command. In an age when the common soldier was regarded as an expendable peasant, this was a radical idea. The Prussian drillmaster was introducing a concept as revolutionary as the Yankees' cause itself.

Without quite knowing it, the Army of the United States was not only being born, it was coming of age as well.

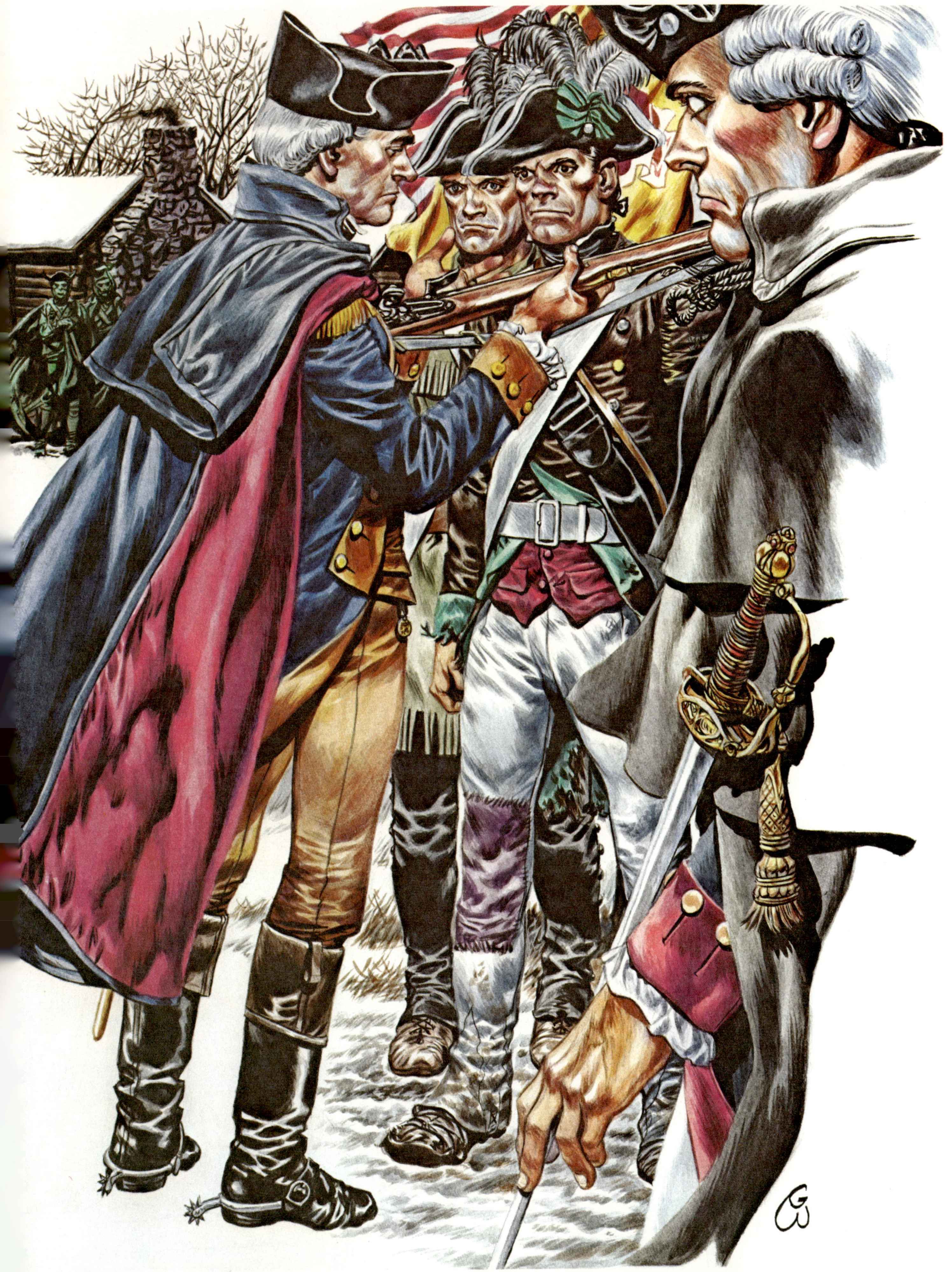

THE LISTENING LADY

One of the most difficult problems facing any army, no matter how professional, is that of keeping its intentions secret while operating in territory peopled by a predominantly hostile population. The spy may be man, woman, or child; may be any of countless sullen faces seeming to ignore the conqueror's presence. The eyes which watch and interpret the daily comings and goings of officers, the arrivals of couriers, the shifting of regiments, the unavoidable public functioning of an occupying garrison, may be those of a single individual or a highly organized clandestine network. The spy requires no elaborate materiel of war. Courage and patience are enough.

The efficiency of the Continental Army's intelligence service was to be a thorn in the side of British commanders throughout the Revolution. This silent service was already functioning effectively by the time the English Army had settled itself snugly in Philadelphia, content to contemplate its string of early victories, while waiting for the icy horrors of Valley Forge to further reduce the shattered remnants of Washington's Army.

☆☆

The patrol of McLane's Horse stopped on the frozen road. They knew they were within a couple of miles of Sir William Howe's pickets keeping watch on the road to Philadelphia. The thought of the British, warm and well fed in the seat of their Congress, was always a bitter one. None of them had dined very well since their last foraging expedition into Maryland. That time they'd come upon a party of British cavalry on a similar mission. Since the troopers of George III paid with hard specie, farmers managed to find the best of provisions for them, while Washington's Army, with its paper money, seemed always to find the larder bare. After some acts of calculated violence by McLane's horsemen had prompted the British to execute a strategic withdrawal, the farmer in whose barnyard the melee had taken place, found himself unable to think of an adequate reason why the Pennsylvanians shouldn't commandeer the produce already loaded in the British wagons. Unfortunately, that had been too long ago.

The troop's current assignment made such enterprises impossible. Its commander, Captain Allan McLane, had been entrusted with the intelligence mission of keeping Sir William's movements under surveillance. In addition to ceaseless patrolling, this involved the use of agents within the city. The spot where the cavalry troopers had halted was one of the several rendezvous kept daily in case an agent had something to report.

The cold air carried the sound of hoofbeats clearly. The troopers loosened their sabers, looked at the priming in their carbines, and waited. Through the bare trees masking a bend in the road, a light gig became visible. Its side curtains were down, keeping off the wind and concealing the driver. The horse was a sedate mare which picked its way delicately between the frozen ruts. The troopers relaxed.

Allan McLane cantered forward, saluting casually. The vehicle stopped as the American officer came alongside. The curtain was pulled aside. The sole occupant was a woman in the sober gray of the Quakers. Her report was crisp—professional. Nominally, Lydia Darrah was a sedate, retiring housewife, a model member of the sober Society of Friends. The one minor flaw in her otherwise spotless character was curiosity, a weakness and a talent which had proved useful to the patriotic cause when Sir William Howe's adjutant general had selected the Darrah home for his own quarters.

She'd been ordered to retire early the previous night. After waiting a respectable period, she'd sneaked on stocking feet to a closed parlor door and listened. She'd heard Howe and his staff officers planning a surprise night attack on General Washington's main force at Whitemarsh.

In the morning she'd obtained permission to leave the city to buy flour at a mill near the rendezvous. Now, she must get back before she became suspect. As her mare began picking its way back along the rutted road, she didn't look back. She knew that McLane and his ragged troopers were already gone.

That night the British columns moving silently through the frosty countryside were hit by a ferocious cavalry charge at Three Mile Run. Disconcerted and confused, the British halted their advance and dressed for battle. Then, as they probed cautiously forward, they were hit again and again. Eventually, Howe's tired battalions reached Chestnut Hill, only to find the American main force waiting for them, and obviously ready for a fight. Two days of indecision led to a fierce firefight, in which McLane's ragamuffin troopers played a major role.

Finally, Howe elected to fall back on Philadelphia; not only was it vastly more comfortable than the frozen countryside, but it offered less exposure to humiliation as well.

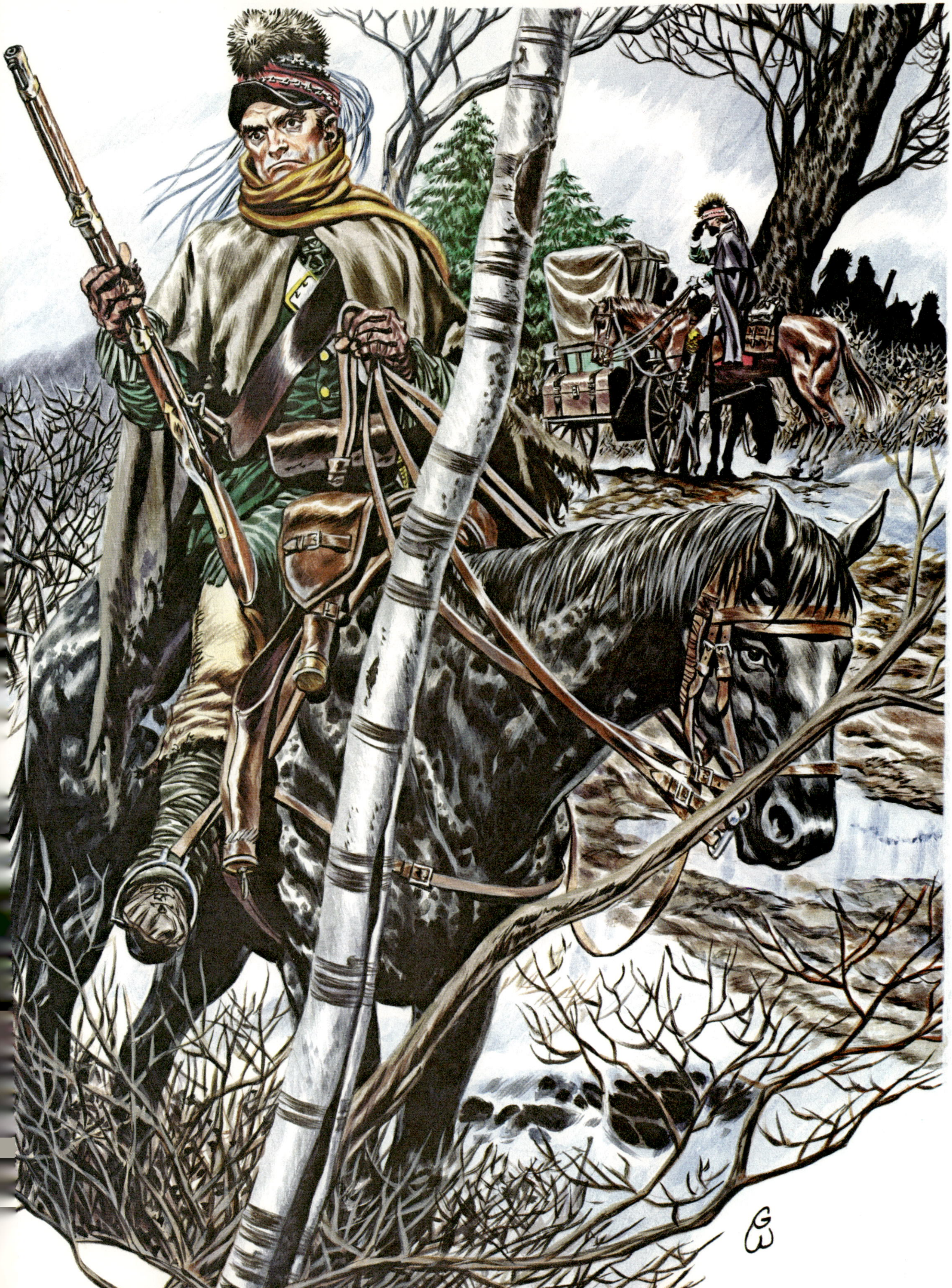

THE UNEXPECTING VICTOR

A newborn state still fighting for its existence is a prime target for the adventurous. Some come to serve; some to profit by it. Often these bring with them formidable reputations, both real and fancied. Mostly, they're soldiers, many mercenaries; a rare few, idealists. The harried leaders of revolutions must choose between self-serving accounts of campaigns won, and of cities taken—usually in very far places—and then hope fervently that they have selected wisely. All too often the choice lies between some glamorous foreigner, sanctified by fabled victories over legendary foes, and some local soldier whose shortcomings are all too well-known and exaggerated.

General George Washington was one so measured. The Continental Congress seemed to be dazzled by the reputation of his nominal second in command. General Charles Lee was a veteran of not only the British armies, but of half the others on the continent of Europe—a man mindful of his own worth and not averse to mentioning his talents to any who would listen.

☆☆

Lieutenant Colonel William Smith was an earnest young man. His family was among Boston's most solid. John Adams would never have approved him as a son-in-law otherwise. He'd been a devoted champion of the American cause since Bunker Hill, an event three years before which seemed like a faint memory now.

It was hard for William to recall when he had not been a soldier, a defeated soldier. He'd gained his rank as so many men of the Revolution did, by distinguishing himself in one retreat after another. He had thought that at last the tide was turning. Trenton, Saratoga, the Army's survival through the winter at Valley Forge, and now Sir Henry Clinton's decision to evacuate Philadelphia and retreat to the comparative safety of New York. The British had been thrown into a near panic by the horrifying news of Burgoyne's surrender and the subsequent entry of France into the conflict on the Yankees' side. The British columns were hurrying across New Jersey by forced marches.

It had been a golden opportunity for General Washington's Continental veterans to even a few old scores, but from the first, there had been an uneasiness in the American regiments. General Charles Lee's orders to his officers hadn't been the most straightforward. These were young commanders whose distrust of the British mercenary was based on his part in the Conway cabal to replace Washington.

Despite his misgivings, Colonel Smith had never expected such a debacle. At Monmouth Courthouse, the British had turned to bloody their harassing pursuers. Smith's regiment, a unit of Brigadier General Anthony Wayne's division, had been spoiling for a fight. Then the incredible had happened! The American army, without a firefight of any consequence, was in full retreat. In the young colonel's eyes, it looked like a rout.

His regiment had made contact with the British, but they'd sustained only one casualty. Then, Smith discovered his flank had been exposed by the withdrawal of the adjoining unit. Enraged and disappointed, he'd ordered his own regiment to fall back.

But the day's shocks were just beginning. Once assured that his companies were withdrawing in good order, Colonel Smith took note of the surrounding battlefield. He noted a cluster of horsemen on the dirt road ahead. They wore the buff and blue of American senior officers. With a shock he recognized a heavily built man mounted on a big white horse. It was Washington, the commander in chief himself. Incredibly, the grave, distant general, usually so formally correct, was roaring angrily. Smith caught one furious phrase, "Damned poltroon"!

Then, spurring his horse, Washington thundered past, shouting a command. Smith couldn't make it out above the roar of approval from his men, but the meaning was obvious. The Virginian swung his saber in an overhead arc, the traditional signal meaning "Follow me." The Bostonian felt a great weight lift from him. It was almost with joy that he shouted the commands which brought his regiment about, prepared to fight.

In the confused, ferocious fight which followed, none of the young Continental officers could spare the time to pity an ignored General Charles Lee sitting his horse amid the debris of his reputation as the best strategist in the Continental Army.

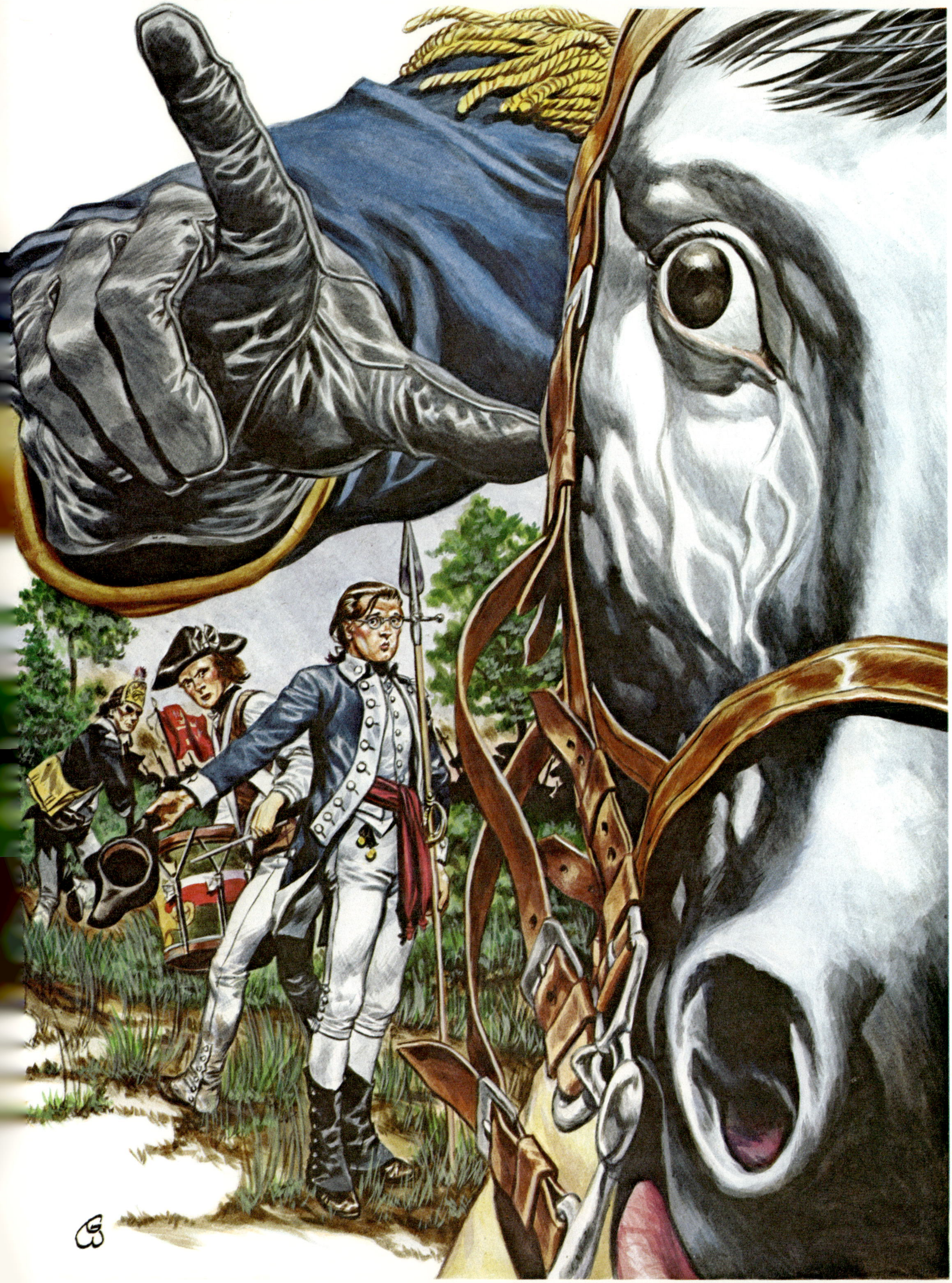

THE PRISONER

Long after a new, sovereign nation's existence has become an accomplished fact, it is not unusual for the state against which it rebelled to be unable to face facts. It seeks to deny the new political reality by pretending that nothing has changed, that the revolt is simply an internal civil disturbance.

This reluctance to face actuality was a rigid article of faith in the governmental councils of the British Empire. The inability to admit that the North American colonies had successfully thrown off London's authority was carried to such lengths as denying the legitimacy of ranks held by officers of the Continental Army on the ground that the American Congress did not have the power to confer them. Even the commander in chief of the United States was referred to in communications between British authorities as "Mister" Washington. Of a more serious nature was the British refusal to treat captured Yankees as honorable prisoners of war, entitled to military usage customary at the time.

☆☆

The blow sent Thomas Andros sprawling. The other prisoners stirred resentfully for an instant, then all too well aware of the hopelessness of their position, resumed their dispirited shuffle toward the hatchway whose foul stench gave dire promise of the hell below. Thousands of American seamen, privateersmen mostly, had already died aboard the British prison ship *Jersey* in New York Harbor. Thousands more would. It took a cautious man to survive.

Thomas Andros staggered weakly to his feet. There was a piercing pain in his side, where the guard's gun butt had taken him. The man wore the green jacket of the British Tory regiments. "Billy, the Ram" was notorious for his sadism. He grinned at Andros. The guards were given considerable latitude in how they enforced discipline among the prisoners. Andros managed to make it to the hatchway.

Out of sight on the ladder below, Thomas Dring and young Christopher Hawkins off the Providence brig, *Mariamne* (taken by two British frigates), were waiting. They helped Andros the rest of the way down into the stinking hold. The only light was from the rows of barred openings cut into the bulkheads above the sealed-up gun ports. Shadowy spectres, emaciated and filthy, made room for them between the planks which served as bunks. These had been able seamen, once. They remembered the necessity of discipline. They understood it was all they had to save themselves from becoming animals.

Andros found that with an effort, he could speak. "Captain Young? They found him, eh?" Dring nodded. "They gave him a hundred with the cat. He died on the grating." Hawkins took up the report. "It was Spicer betrayed him. Both of us being from Providence, he told me. The Lobsterbacks promised him a bosun's berth aboard a Tory coaster if he informed." The privateersmen glanced at each other. There was no need to discuss the matter further. They knew what had to be done. Captain Young had been a valuable man to the American cause. Much time and effort had gone into planning his escape.

The next night prisoner Spicer was pushed off the gangway as the men were being driven below decks by the guards. He managed to scream once, before they killed him. The British weren't concerned enough to mete out any punishment.

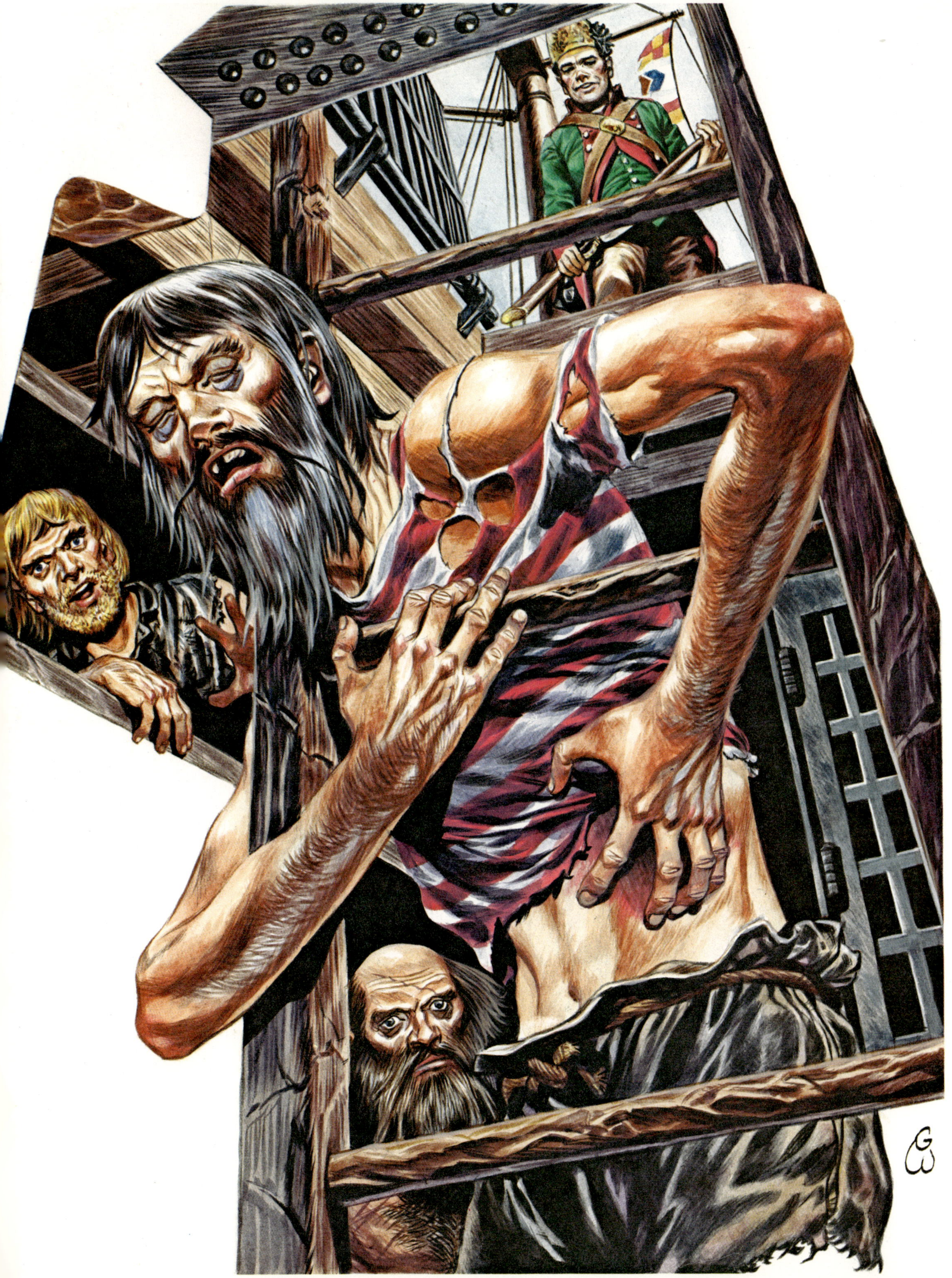

THE BLUFFING GAMBLER

The random patterns by which revolutions develop are often the consequence of an inexperienced leadership, unable to control all facets of an expanding area of combat, and ignoring situations of vital importance to the future of the people they are trying to guide. This can result in a few men, operating under the vaguest of orders, or even on their own initiative, taking actions which will be of the greatest consequence to their infant nation.

This state of affairs had come about in the vast reaches of the North American continent west of the last English-speaking outposts of the new American republic. The area had been sparsely settled by the French. Now, under the nominal jurisdiction of the British governor of Canada, it was both a barrier to westward expansion by the Americans and a menace to their security. The American Congress, fighting for survival, could do nothing but leave its fate up to a handful of frontier militiamen.

☆☆

Captain Leonard Helms of the Virginia Militia stood in the stockade gateway of the palisaded fort at Vincennes, Indiana Territory, and blew on a linstock. The fieldpiece beside him was aimed to sweep the dirt road approaches to the gate with canister. Its presence had been noted by the cluster of British officers and Indian war chiefs watching from just beyond range.

To British General Hamilton and his staff officers as well as the native allies, the lone American and his cannon seemed more of a puzzle than an obstacle. When his column had left Detroit intent on recapturing the former French settlements which Colonel George Rogers Clark (operating under orders from Patrick Henry, governor of Virginia) had been acquiring in wholesale lots, Vincennes had been the prime prize of all the towns along the Wabash. Hamilton had expected that Clark would have strongly garrisoned the fortified town. The lone figure in the distant gateway was, unbelievably, the only American who'd so far shown himself. The British command was uneasily suspicious of a trap.

The answer to General Hamilton's problem was too simple to be taken seriously. The sixty-year-old Kentucky frontiersman *was* alone. The British commander would have been skeptical if he'd been informed that Colonel Clark's Virginia strike force had never been more than an outsize combat patrol. He'd left Redstone, Pennsylvania, with 200 men. This small force had been able to move fast enough to achieve surprise. By spreading word of the new French alliance, Clark had won over the local townspeople, making resistance negligible. However, in order to hold the towns, Clark was compelled to spread his force perilously thin. He'd left a garrison at Vincennes—Captain Helms and five Americans with the doubtful support of twenty French militiamen.

General Hamilton, arriving in the Territory with a much superior force, had forced Helms to make a difficult decision. Obviously, he could not hold Vincennes with five men. The French civilians, pawns in a struggle for empire wherein they no longer had a stake, would sensibly reaffirm their allegiance to King George as quickly as they'd foresworn it when the Americans arrived. It had seemed to Helms that the only course he still had open was to save the five first-class frontier fighting men of his garrison. In Clark's campaign, no man was expendable. First, Helms had them wheel his small French brass fieldpiece into position and surround it with a supply of powder, shot, food, and Monongahela whiskey. Then, he'd ordered them to move out and link up with Clark's main column.

Now, leaning comfortably on his cannon, linstock glowing, Helms sipped the raw mountain whiskey appreciatively and bought time for his troops to get safely away. He'd been in position for several hours and was reasonably sure that his men were beyond reach of the British's Indian patrols. Time was not dealing so kindly with General Hamilton. Indecisiveness was a trait not much admired by his Indian allies. Eventually, unless the impasse was solved, they'd be tempted into either an impulsive assault, or a spontaneous retreat. Either way, they would lose their respect for him, his only hold on their loyalties.

Leonard Helms, who'd spent much of his life among these same Indians, was well aware of Hamilton's dilemma. He was therefore not surprised when he saw a scarlet-coated, mounted figure detach itself from the distant group and canter deliberately toward him. The dark blue facings of his regimentals indicated that the rider was a British general—Hamilton, himself. Evidently the lieutenant governor was not personally a coward.

The little brass cannon could kill the Englishman, but the Indians would then have an excuse to massacre the people of the town. Helms was as much a captive of circumstances as Hamilton. The bluff had worked well enough to save the five Americans, but now the bluff was pointless. Hamilton was steeling himself against the possibility that the forbidding figure in the gateway would raise his linstock to the touchhole of the fieldpiece when he became aware that the fellow was cordially offering him a bottle, still half-filled with some noxious-smelling spirits.

Along the Atlantic seaboard great battles would decide the future of the new republic, but beyond the Alleghenies, a few dozen men, by force and guile, gave it room to expand into a great power.

64

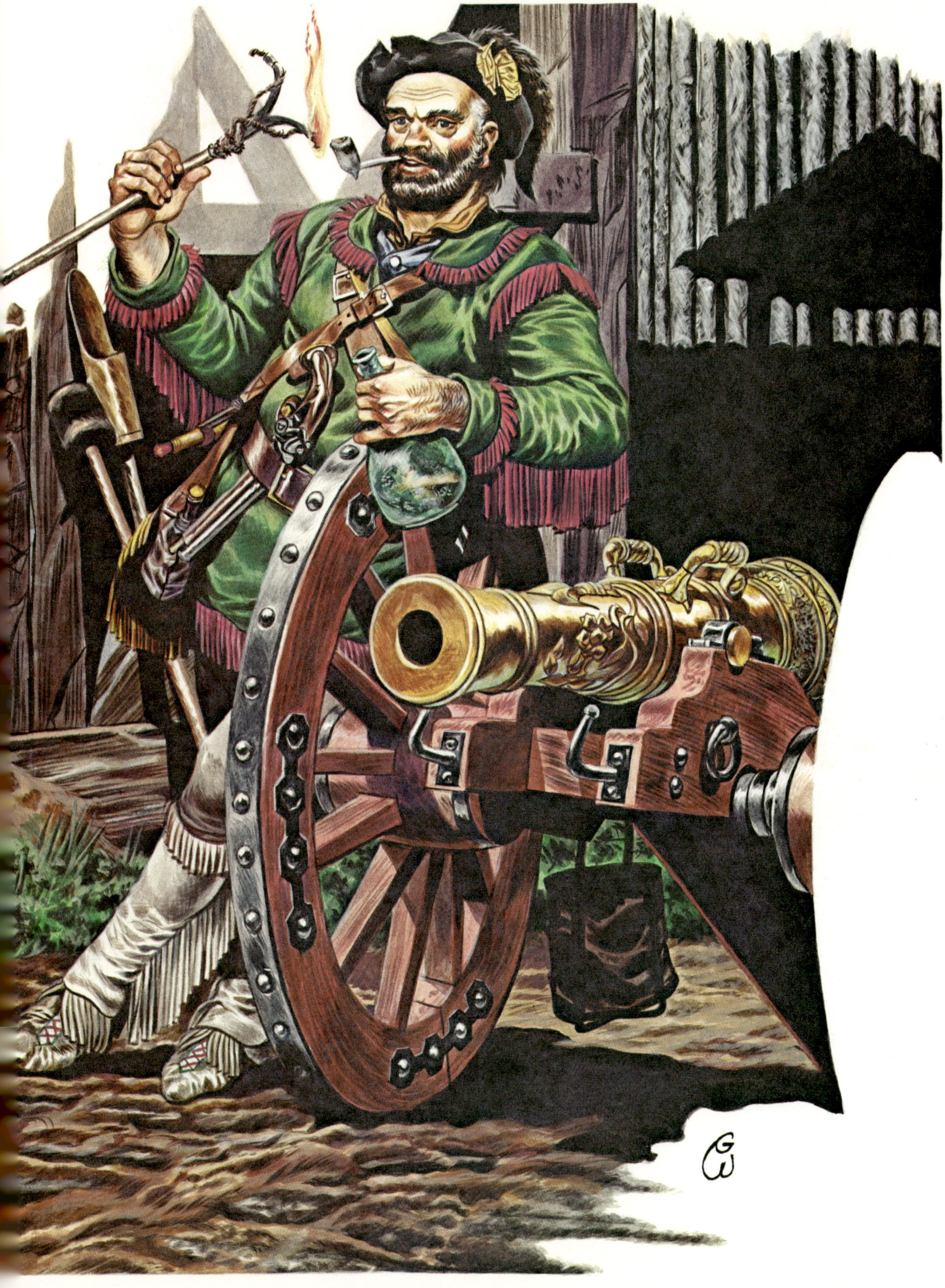

THE NEW ELITE

The armed forces of a new nation born in conflict begin their existence at a disadvantage. Not only is the officer corps inexperienced on the whole in the practice of leadership, but its common soldier comes to battle without a full realization of its total horror, and without the stiffening influence of veterans around him. In a protracted war, he then finds himself with few options. If his pride or patriotism will not allow him to defect, he must learn his terrible new trade simply in order to survive. Those who come through the schooling will be excellent soldiers. Not only have they learned the fighting skills, but—still fired by the ideals which brought them to the revolt in the beginning—they are now both dedicated and professional.

The Army of the United States began to show such a metamorphosis. By the late summer of 1779, the rank and file of the Continental line regiments had marched and fought a long way from the haphazard grouping of impulsive civilians who'd first gathered beyond the British defense works around Boston.

☆☆☆

The two American officers stood quietly watching, as the light infantry picked its way through the film of tidewater over Sandy Point. This would be the acid test of Inspector General von Steuben's training. Ahead, overawing in the dim light, stood Stony Point. It glowered over the Hudson River like some massive threat, which it was; one hundred and fifty feet of bare, rocky promontory, crowned by the British fortification and girdled by its double abatis. Most of the American high command thought this effort was madness, but General Washington trusted the judgment of Brigadier General Anthony Wayne. Both Wayne and his deputy, Colonel Richard Butler, knew that they must not fail at the night's business.

The battle plan was daring, bordering on reckless. Never before had American troops closed with British, those masters of cold steel, without rounds in their muskets. Still, this was Wayne's approach to a silent night attack. Surprise must be complete. No military force could scale that cold, shelterless, rocky ridge if the defenders were sweeping it with canister from their emplaced batteries. As an added hazard, the British warship *Vulture* was lying just off the bank.

As the last of the infantry slipped by, the two officers saluted silently and parted, each hurrying to his own command. Wayne was sending his people up the rocks in two columns, one under his own command, the other under Butler.

They were ghostly in the darkness, moving cautiously, knee-deep in water. Now, the vanguard was beginning to climb—one hundred and fifty men, each armed with a heavy logger's axe. They were at the first tangle of timbers and sharp-pointed logs before the British sentry on the crest heard them.

His bellow of alarm was justified. The Continental light infantry made an unnerving sight as they darted up the slope, their bayonets gleaming wickedly. Ahead of them, the axemen swung their blades frantically, hacking paths through the abatis.

Lieutenant Colonel Johnson, the British garrison commander, found himself in a confusing situation. He was unable to believe that the Americans were ready to risk a cold steel confrontation with his blooded veteran grenadiers, well-known for their proficiency at that gory business. He elected to send his line battalions, half his infantry strength, to meet the Americans at the abatis. He'd scarcely committed them when musket fire sounded from another quarter. With no way of knowing that this was a single American company creating a diversion, he deployed his grenadier companies to meet what he assumed would be the main assault. He was wrong.

The American light infantry streamed through the breached abatis at a dozen points. Overwhelmed, the British companies fell back. The Americans gave them no time to execute their withdrawal in good order. With the grenadiers immobilized, the line companies disintegrated. Before Johnson could restore his defenses, the Americans were over the parapet. For a few moments, there was resistance by a part of the British 17th Foot, holding out in the central log barracks. Then all resistance collapsed.

Not only had Von Steuben's methods worked, but in the hands of a resourceful commander like "Mad Anthony" Wayne, the Continentals had become the equal of Britain's best.

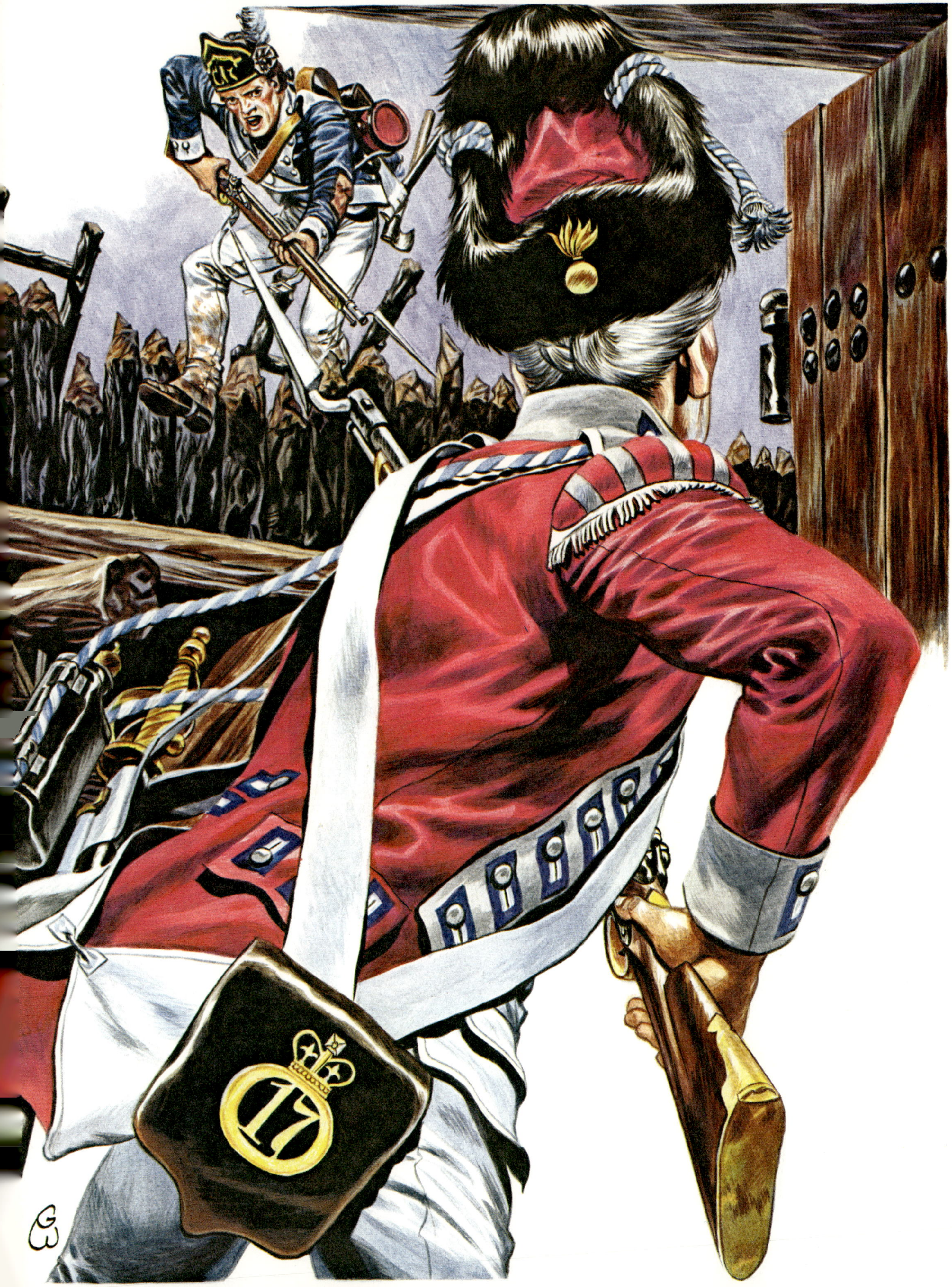
17

THE UNEXPECTED GUNNER

One of the humiliations the leadership of an inadequately equipped new nation at war learns bitterly is that what cannot be mended must be endured. This makes for an extra degree of satisfaction when later circumstances make possible the settling of old scores.

Having been forced almost helplessly for years to endure ravages by the Iroquois Nation (led by ruthless Tory commanders) on the western frontier, the American Congress was agreeably pleased when a stalemate developed in the main theaters of operations. At this point, Sir Henry Clinton in New York was planning a new southern strategy to replace the bankrupt northern campaigns.

☆☆☆

Captain Machin checked the position of his battery with loving care. No one would ever be able to measure the sweat, muscle, and vulgarities required to transport these four-pounders through the trackless forests of the Iroquois country of western York state.

The expeditionary forces of 3000 Continentals and militia under General John Sullivan was under orders to destroy the home bases of the Indians whom Chief Joseph Brant and the Tory, John Butler, had led on one massacre after another throughout the frontier.

The lack of movement by the British Army had made it possible for Washington to risk the precious veteran troops necessary for such a mission. After the usual delays and disappointments, Sullivan's force had caught up with Butler's main body. It consisted of nearly a thousand Iroquois, with a strong contingent of Tory Rangers and a handful of British Regulars.

They'd attempted an ambush of the American column in a narrow defile of the Chemung River Valley, but Sullivan's reconnaissance patrols had spotted it. Butler had established his line astutely, with a strong detachment holding a hill on his right to avoid being outflanked. However, Sullivan had managed to work his artillery and a protective screen of infantry in a circling movement which put them in Butler's rear.

To Machin, it seemed the Tory commander was trying to protect the large Indian settlement known to the whites as "New Town." He suspected the Royalist would have chosen to retreat, if he'd known of the artillery.

The fighting on the frontier had mostly been a matter of rifle or musket, bayonet and tomahawk, pistol and scalping knife. While cannon were to be expected in the widely scattered forts, they were rarely found in the field.

Captain Machin hoped profoundly that his four-pounders would wreak havoc. He'd heard what Butler's Iroquois had done at the Wyoming massacre and German Flats. On top of that, word had finally reached the artilleryman that his hometown of Kingston, York state, had been burned to the ground by a frustrated General Henry Clinton, retreating after his abortive attempt to link up with General Burgoyne.

Satisfied that his pieces were on target, he looked back and signalled. An answering signal was given and the little guns roared mightily. His ranging shots thudded home into the Royalist entrenchments. For the next half hour, his cannon fired as rapidly as they could be served. Then, the "Cease Fire" was passed. Cautiously, the infantry moved forward. Then they were in the entrenchments and it was evident that the enemy had pulled out.

A black slave of one of the Tory officers had taken the occasion to secure his freedom by hiding out until Butler's force had vanished into the forest. He told the Americans that the Indians had broken first. Never under cannon fire before, they'd panicked. The Tory Rangers and British Regulars had been swept up in the rout.

The easy victory put the Continentals in a jovial mood. When it was established that the body count added up to twelve dead Iroquois braves and one squaw, Machin found himself embarrassed by a flood of rude witticisms commenting on his furious bombardment and its meager results.

He needn't have been. The cannonading had cast such terror into the Iroquois that never again would they oppose American troops with artillery. In addition, Sullivan's campaign so devastated the Iroquois country that in the coming winter they would have to be fed by the British, a burden rather than an asset.

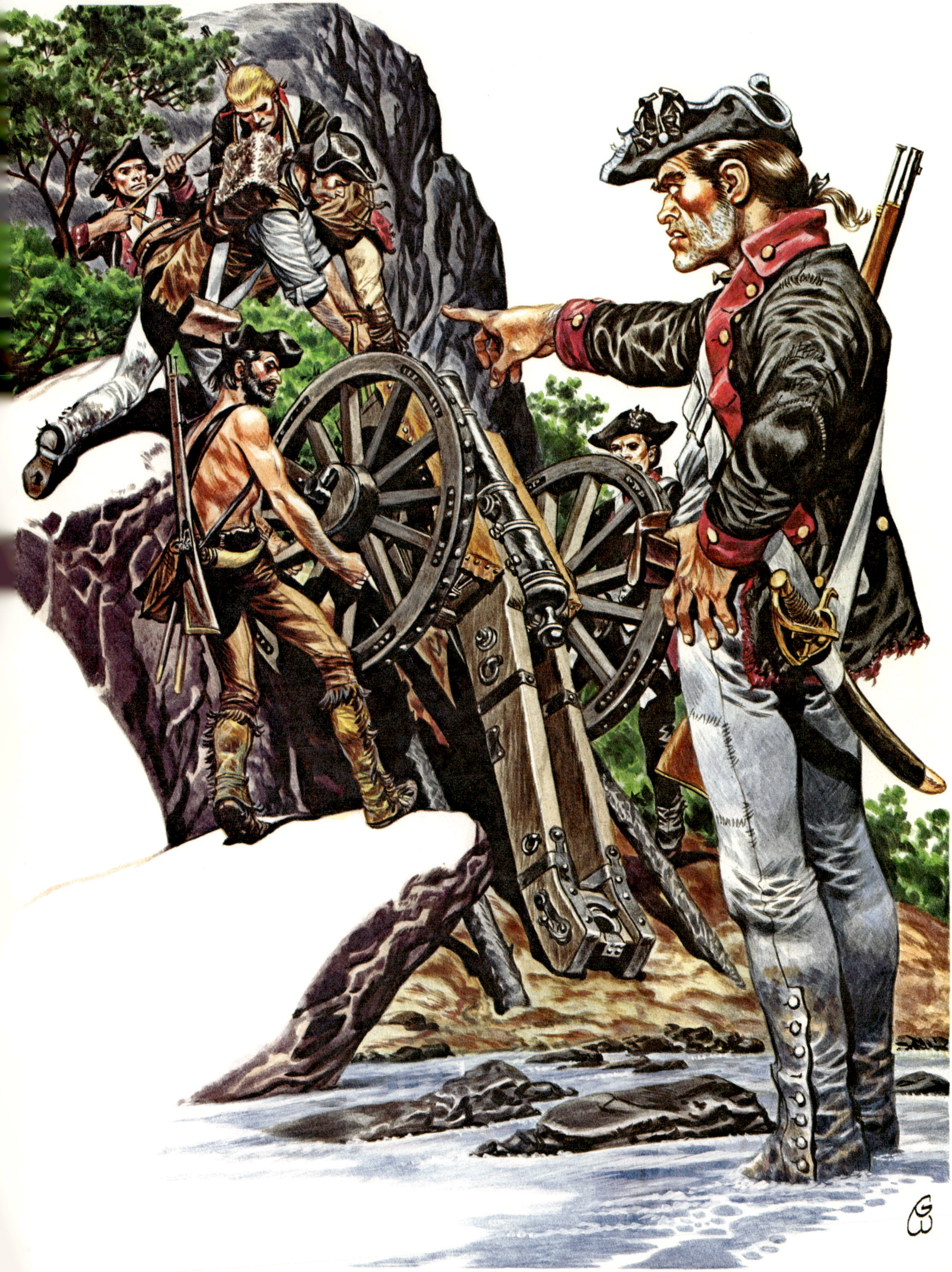

THE KINDRED SPIRIT

There is an emotional quality in the struggle of a young nation to establish itself as an independent political entity which stirs especially the minds of those who've fought similar battles. So they come to join the fight along with the mercenaries and the adventurers—not out of regard for the embattled citizenry, but in response to the dictates of their own convictions.

The rebels of the former British colonies in North America found themselves playing host to a distinguished group of such libertarians. Surprisingly, most of them were aristocrats. But these were the new men. Fired by Voltaire and the other prophets of the Age of Reason, they were in revolt against the interlocking feudal establishment which governed Europe regardless of national boundaries. Many of them had already fought for (and all of them wished for) a new society. Their contribution was to become invaluable.

☆☆

The two foreign officers sat their horses and stared bleakly at the city of Savannah, Georgia. Count Casimir Pulaski was only half-hearing his senior. He was already familiar with the French admiral's reasoning. The Comte d'Estaing proposed a frontal assault against the British of Major General Augustine Prevost who were solidly entrenched in and around the town. Count Pulaski knew it couldn't be done without taking substantial losses. The British engineers had been busy. Their first obstacle was a tangle of sharpened tree trunks woven into an impenetrable mass. Beyond were field entrenchments, supported by redoubts situated to give enfilading fire.

Pulaski wondered where the American General Lincoln was—their theater commander. Any experienced land strategist would realize that the proper tactic called for a siege while sappers undermined the strong points and barriers. Then, after a proper softening up, a saturation cannonade, followed by an infantry attack, and the job would be done. Unfortunately, d'Estaing was a seaman. He was worried about his ships. He wanted Savannah taken quickly so that he could reembark his infantry regiments and get his fleet out into open water before the rumors of a prowling British fleet were proved true.

The Polish cavalryman, Congress's chief of cavalry, was not especially happy with his own troops. He'd raised his legion himself, when he realized that Washington, an infantryman, would not employ cavalry to any serious extent in this war. The pool of available manpower had not been outstanding. His officers were European mercenaries, the troopers mostly British deserters. He'd have preferred the squadrons of Polish lancers he'd earlier commanded in the foredoomed war against Russian domination of his homeland, but this ragtag legion would have to serve. The safety of the French fleet could not be jeopardized.

The drums and fifes signalled the attack. Count Pulaski put his horse into a gentle canter. The 200 troopers at his heels seemed pitifully few as they moved out. At the abatis they came within range of the British guns. Frantically, officers spurred their horses along the edges of the obstruction, seeking a weak spot where horses could jump through to the other side. Now, troopers were pitching out of their saddles as the Tory riflemen in the supporting redoubt found the range. Some of the legionnaires began drifting back. Angrily, Pulaski realized that his charge was broken unless he rallied his followers quickly. Signalling with his saber, he urged his mount into the obstruction. A cluster of horsemen followed.

He'd nearly broken through into the clear when the distant sniper's round found him. It was purely professional pride which made the handful of deserters and tavern commandos pause long enough to retrieve him before they fled.

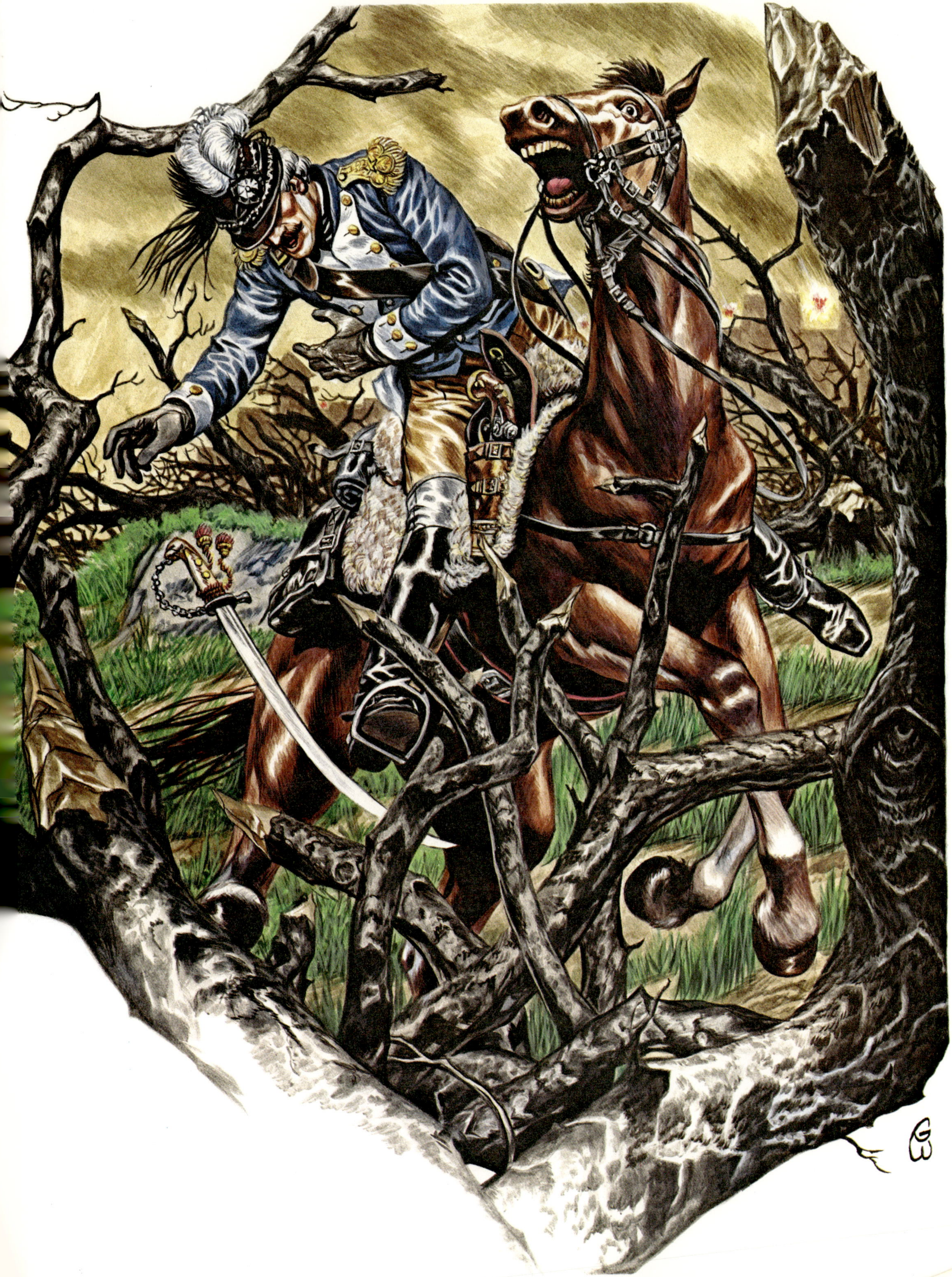

THE RECKLESS PRAGMATIST

As it does in most human endeavors, luck plays a considerable part in determining the outcome of the gambles revolutionists must risk. The hazards of the American revolt were no exception.

It was inevitable that since both Great Britain and her former colonies were maritime powers, they would clash on sea as well as land. The infant United States had no chance of matching the mighty Royal Navy, gun for gun. However, she had no shortage of daring seamen. Although unable to breach the blockade of American harbors, they were able to interpose a counterblockade of the British home islands which forced the English merchant fleet to sail in slow, unwieldy convoys, despite which the ships were seldom safe. It made bitter men of London's merchant princes. This was accomplished with some 2000 privateers and a small fleet of far-ranging United States Navy raiders.

☆☆

William Hamilton was in a towering Celtic rage. He'd sailed under John Paul Jones convinced that a canny fellow Scot would never get so carried away as to act recklessly. As a regularly enlisted seaman in the newly formed United States Navy and an unforgiving enemy of the English, he was firmly convinced that the Sassenach should be punished for their assorted high crimes. However, he preferred that this be done in a sensible manner.

He'd been well pleased with Jones's deportment on the voyage across the Atlantic. He'd approved highly of the taking of prizes by the American ship, *Ranger*. Of late, however, his commanding officer had been downgraded considerably in his estimation. First, there was the matter of transferring to this antique tub, *Bonhomme Richard*; she leaked. Her crew was a polyglot mob of dockside sweepings and the idea of sending her against the British Baltic convoy, guarded by first-rate men-of-war like the *Serapis*, was downright foolhardy. Also, they were accompanied by another American frigate, *Alliance*, commanded by a Frenchman who was either an imbecile or a traitor.

Hamilton's worst forebodings had been fulfilled. The *Bonhomme Richard* was locked with *Serapis*. The Englishman with her two gun decks had made the old French Indiaman's hulk a bloody shambles. On top of everything else, that crazy Frenchman in *Alliance* was confusedly pouring shot into her from the opposite side. Of the two French ships sailing with them, the *Pallas* had taken the *Countess of Scarborough* and was so overcome with her good fortune that she'd dropped out of the fight. Her sister ship, *Vengeance*, had disappeared completely as soon as the sea fight began.

Hamilton, along with most of the surviving Americans, had swarmed up the *Richard*'s ratlines to avoid the deadly hail of grape, canister, and langrage sweeping her decks from *Serapis*'s batteries. This had turned out well. From their perches in the fighting tops, they could pick off any British seaman who showed himself. Unfortunately, they could do nothing about the *Serapis*'s guns, below decks, still reducing the American hulk to kindling.

Then Hamilton had an idea. It was the sort of thought which any rational human being would regard as impractical, but Hamilton's indignation was monumental. He'd noted a bucket of grenades, part of the top's usual armament. Still calling down the wrath of remote Celtic spirits on all fools including himself, he'd crawled out on a main yard and was now above the Englishman's deck. Locating an open hatchway, he was bent on showing the English how uncomfortable high explosives could be in a crowded gun deck.

Hitting as small a target as that open hatchway was no small matter. The Scot missed several times before he became lucky. He gave a roar of satisfaction as the grenade vanished into the dark hole. The result was awe-inspiring. For once, William Hamilton was astounded by his own efforts. The hatchway had led to *Serapis*'s powder magazine.

Half an hour later, aboard the captured English frigate, Hamilton had watched the *Bonhomme Richard* go down. With the rest of the American crew, he'd herded the British seamen below decks aboard their own vessel. Then, ignoring the general self-congratulation indulged in by his mates, he'd dourly reflected that his foolhardy commander, Paul Jones, would get all the credit. He was right.

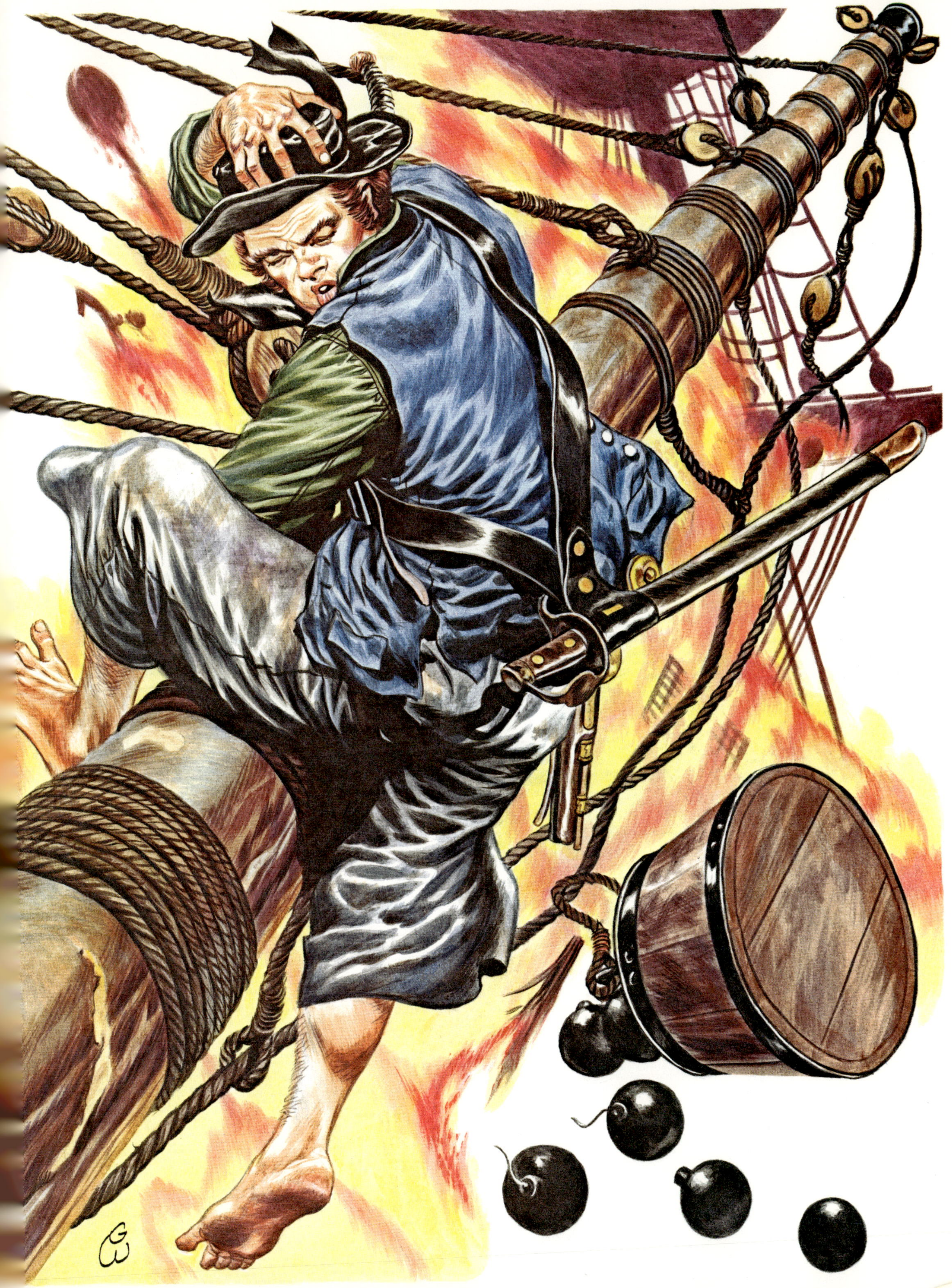

THE DEADLY ANTAGONISTS

To a new nation, totally involved in its problems of immediate survival, it is possible for an event of dramatic promise to pass unnoticed.

It is doubtful if the members of the American Congress or their military commanders realized that the British dispatch of Lord Cornwallis and a considerable body of troops to the southern states signalled the complete failure of England's northern strategy. The master plan to divide the colonies had died at Saratoga. General Clinton, overextended, had even been compelled to leave Philadelphia to the Rebels and hole up in New York. Still, to the Americans, a campaign in the South must have seemed like one more tribulation with which they must somehow cope.

Certainly General Washington, hoarding his seasoned veterans of the Continental Line, could not risk weakening his watch on Clinton's main battle group, licking its wounds in Manhattan Island. However, what could be done was done. General Gates, with such regiments as could be spared from the main theater, was ordered south. Beyond that, the southern states were compelled to rely on their own resources. It was fortunate for the United States that those resources included some very able fighting men.

☆☆☆

Colonel Francis Marion sat very still in his saddle. Around him, the darkness was taut with that special silence where tense, armed men are hiding and waiting. Even the sound—muffled, menacing—from the dense brush beyond the open glade prompted nothing more than a whispered reassurance from a trooper to his skittish horse.

Then the pursuing cavalry came into view. A hundred or more riders, their green jackets and dark helmets part of the night, leaning low, spurring their horses. Even the sound of hooves was muted by the shallow swamp water they disturbed, sent splashing in glittering patterns in the moonlight. They could almost have been shadows, a trick of the yellow moon just above the line of the Carolina bog land.

From their hiding place in the shadows, the Americans could see the pursuing cavalry commander's face clearly. It was red, contorted with anger. There were minor sounds as the troop sped past, the jingle of metal, the creak of leather, the muttering of horsemen urging more speed from their mounts. Then a cloud drifted across the moon. When it had passed, the ghostly squadron had vanished.

Francis Marion allowed himself the luxury of a sardonic grin. This time he'd outwitted Banastre Tarleton. It always gave him an added twinge of pleasure when he could savage Lord Cornwallis' daring cavalry commander and his brutal Tory troopers. The British colonel, whom the people of the Carolinas called the "Butcher," was no abstract opponent, but a personal enemy, cordially hated. The sentiment was returned.

In the distance, there was a mutter of ominous sound and a faint reddish light lit the sky for a mere second. Marion watched it without comment. There were a few cheerful whispers from his troopers. It had been a satisfactory night's work. The glow had come from the final explosion in the burned-out wreckage of a sizable ammunition supply train which would never reach the British force in Charleston. It had been important enough to be convoyed by Colonel Tarleton and his Loyalist legion.

Marion gestured and a trooper sidled his horse to the leader's side. Moments later, with the American guerrilla leader's report committed to memory, the courier was on his way to report to General Gates, commanding the southern department of the Continental Army. Gates's headquarters at Hillsboro would learn of the successful action before morning.

At a softly spoken command, the detachment of Yankee irregulars formed into a column of twos and cantered quietly onto the almost invisible path which would eventually bring them to their secret bivouac. Marion watched them go. They were less than forty men. Until Gates took the field, the state of freedom in the South would depend on pathetic bands such as this. The irregular cavalryman suspected that the stakes were high enough to demand a major commitment eventually. However, until that day, the game belonged to Banastre Tarleton and the "Swamp Fox."

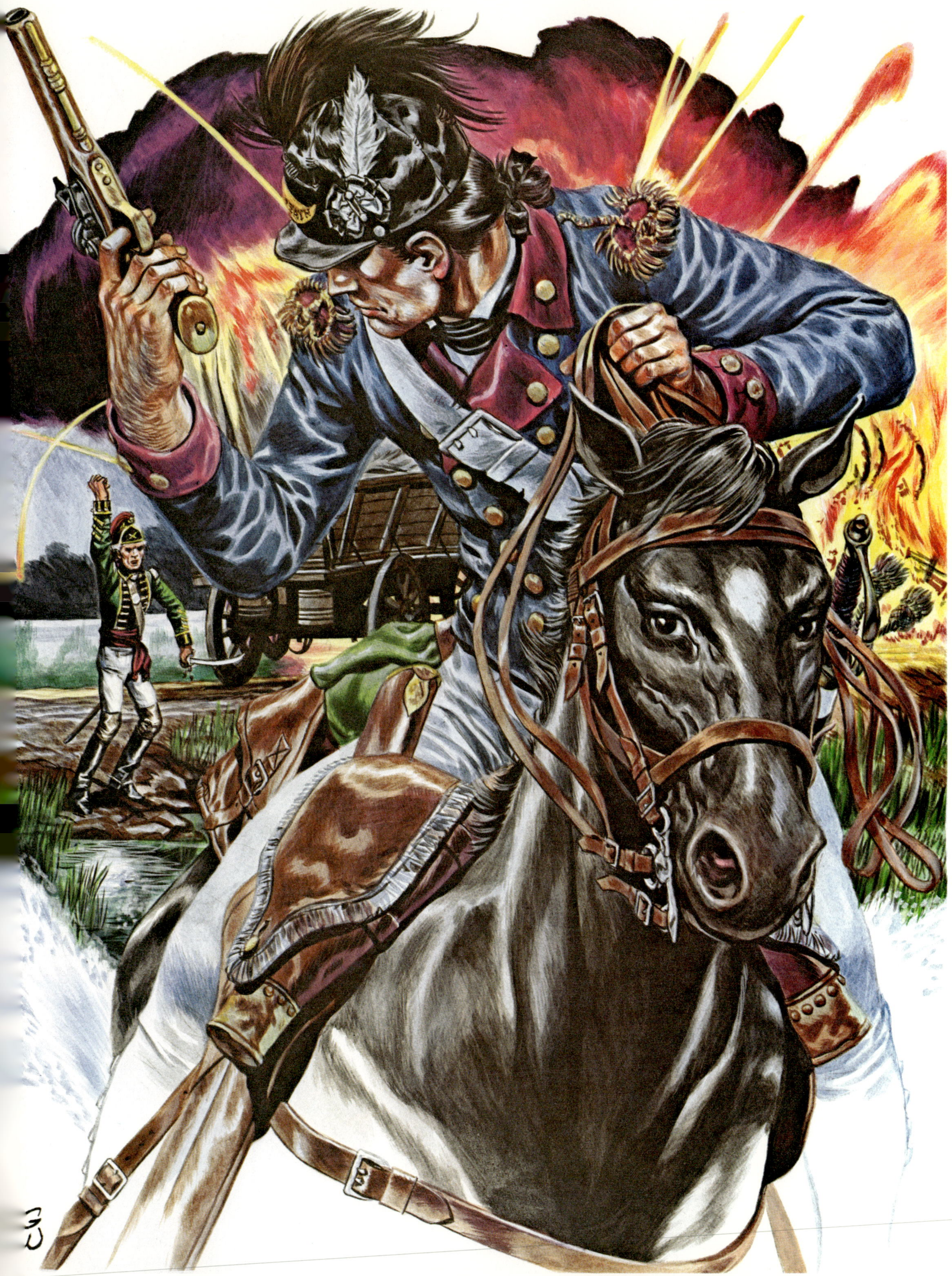

THE INQUISITIVE LADY

It is probably a historical truism that the jury-rigged governments of new nations will make errors. The fight for survival may dictate that it be politically expedient to reward the incompetent, ignore the able, play off clique against clique, and placate those with powerful friends. And, in its insecurity, the new government may never feel free to acknowledge its mistakes.

The British, unable to force a decision on their rebellious colonies by arms, were not unaware of the fact that the inexperienced Congress had made enemies among its own best people, that there were Americans in vital positions whose accomplishments had been poorly rewarded and whose pride had been humiliated. To establish a treasonous agreement with an embittered Rebel whose loyalty had been abraded by wounded vanity might accomplish what the military might of His Britannic Majesty had been unable to do.

☆☆☆☆☆☆☆☆☆☆☆☆☆☆☆☆☆☆☆☆☆☆☆☆☆☆☆☆☆☆☆☆☆☆☆☆☆☆

Sally Townsend was uncomfortably aware that the two British officers in the next room would have been very angry if they'd known she was listening. They would have been even more indignant if they suspected that the son of their host, Mr. Townsend of Raynham Hall in Oyster Bay on Long Island, was the mysterious Culper, Jr., one of General Washington's spies on Manhattan Island, practically in Sir Henry Clinton's private quarters.

Sally Townsend knew that her brother was involved in some sort of clandestine activity on behalf of the Revolution. She'd been discreet enough not to try to find out more, but she was acutely aware of the secret war being fought out beneath the surface in and around New York.

At first she'd thought that she was being melodramatic when she'd noticed a neighbor, supposedly a staunch patriot, leave a folded piece of paper in a kitchen cooky jar. Excited, she'd decided to see what came of it. It had really startled her when Major André, quartered at Raynham Hall, surreptitiously retrieved it and slipped it into a pocket.

Watching Major André, she'd early realized that he seemed to have an odd military duty. He did not command troops, nor did he seem to engage in the routine which usually occupied staff officers. She wished that her brother in New York would make one of his infrequent visits. She thought he'd be interested. He would. She'd identified Sir Henry Clinton's chief of intelligence.

When Lieutenant Colonel Simcoe turned up, she'd thought he was another agent. However, she shortly became satisfied that he was merely a typical cavalry officer, suffering the standard delusion that he was irresistible to women. Personable young men were hard to come by, however, so his obvious attentions to her were tolerated.

As friends, André and Simcoe spent hours talking and joking over a bottle of her father's Madeira. Of late Sally had taken to eavesdropping on them. This time she'd had the usual difficulty in distinguishing what was said, but she'd heard two words clearly, "West Point."

She'd slipped away to her room and scribbled a note. Aware of her attractiveness, she knew she'd have no trouble finding a British officer willing to handcarry a letter to her dear brother on his next trip to New York.

Some time later, Major Tallmadge (2nd Connecticut Dragoons, on detached service as one of General Washington's chief intelligence officers), returning from a front line reconnaissance patrol to the American outpost at North Castle outside New York, was intrigued to learn that a pair of Militiamen had picked up a wandering civilian named "John Anderson." A routine search had uncovered a pass signed by General Arnold, commanding at West Point, which the man had tried to hide. Even more odd, in his boot were discovered documents and letters which seemed to concern Arnold and the defenses at the impregnable fortress on the Hudson.

Colonel Jameson, commanding the American outposts, had found it all confusing and sent the man, under escort, to Washington's headquarters. Tallmadge flung himself back onto his horse and set out in pursuit. Very vividly, he recalled a letter, forwarded by his agent, "Culper, Jr.," from the spy's home on Long Island. Tallmadge knew who Major André was, very well.

Silently, he cursed Jameson. The man should have sent a detail to West Point with orders to intercept the Revolution's most admired general. By now, it was likely too late, but Tallmadge intended to make sure that his intelligence adversary did not slip through his fingers. He admired André's style. It would take the British a long time to suitably replace him. Until they did, the Rebel agents would have a field day.

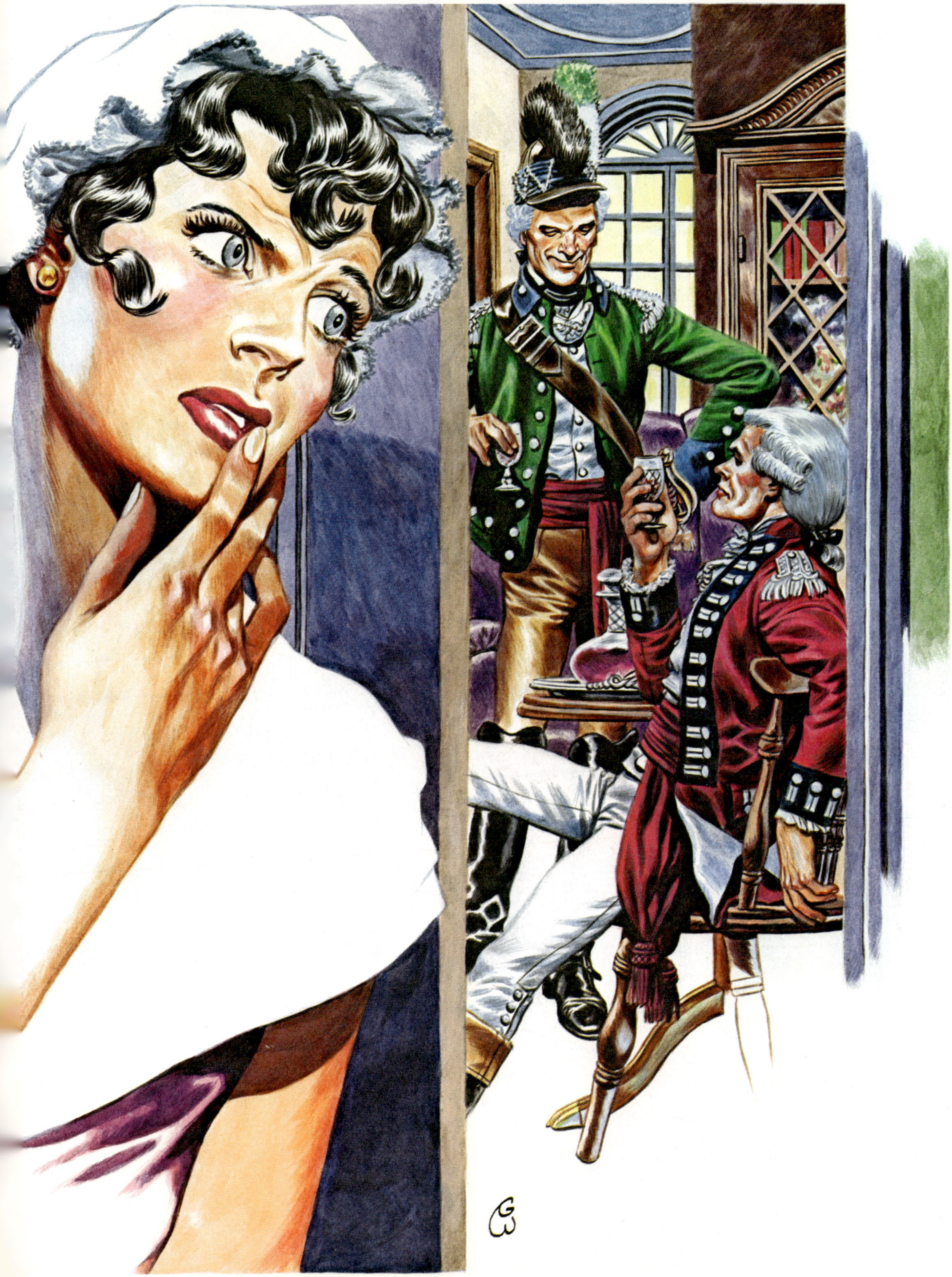

THE TURNCOAT'S TURNCOAT

As a practical matter, no military establishment can afford to tolerate treason. Basically, it is a disciplined society which holds men to their duty under the most trying of circumstances. In general, devotion to one's country and its cause, self-respect and respect for the warrior tradition of the human race are sufficient to motivate its members. However, for any who may be tempted to deviate, fear of punishment and the contempt of one's peers are the other side of the coin which enables the martial organization to function successfully.

These were factors of which General George Washington was well aware in considering the case of Major General Benedict Arnold. In addition, there was the personal hurt. He had trusted and respected the hero of the fighting on the Canadian frontier, of Saratoga, of all the campaigns of the Northern Army. He had personally entrusted to Arnold's hands the responsibility for the massive American fortress at West Point whose presence denied the Hudson Valley to the British. It was a coldly furious commander in chief who consulted with his fellow Virginian, Colonel "Light Horse Harry" Lee.

☆☆

Angrily, John Champe noted how easily Benedict Arnold had taken to the British officer's attitude of casual arrogance in dealing with an inferior. The order he'd given the new sergeant major of his freshly recruited "American Legion" might have been addressed to his valet.

But Champe had more reason than the American traitor's manners to rage inwardly. Saluting smartly, he left the new British brigadier's quarters at number 3 Broadway in the Royalist-held city of New York. He paused in the rear exit and stared somberly at the rear garden within its picket fence and beyond, the black rocks at the Hudson shore which had seemed so convenient for his purpose.

His mission was a failure, wiped out by Arnold's order that the Legion be embarked in the British transports at anchor in the bay. The traitor's luck had held. There would not even be an opportunity to pass the word to Baldwin. His contact and accomplice would have his boat waiting at the old pier among the rocks. Across the river, in the Jersey marshes, the party of Continental dragoons would wait in vain.

Desperately, he hoped that his fellow Virginians, especially Colonel Lee, would figure out what had happened. "Light-Horse Harry" was a keen judge of men. He would understand that his sergeant major had done his best. The troopers of Lee's corps would probably always think he'd deserted, but it couldn't be helped.

Champe had risked his life to desert the American encampment near Totowa, not far from the Great Falls of the Passaic in New Jersey. Now, by sheer chance, the effort had been rendered futile. Worst of all, the new sergeant major of Arnold's Legion would now have to board the British transport with his unit; the destination, Chesapeake Bay. Champe knew the Legion's mission. It was to burn, destroy, lay waste his home state of Virginia. If he attempted to desert from this side and failed, the British would hang him.

About the only sad little positive note to his position, Champe realized, was the fact that he would not be able to report failure in person to General Washington. The ex-Rebel cavalryman considered his former commander in chief a very stern man. It had been General Washington's own idea that Champe pose as a deserter, ingratiate himself with the traitor, Arnold, kidnap him and drag him to the American camp by the heels—there to be publicly tried and ceremoniously hung as an example.

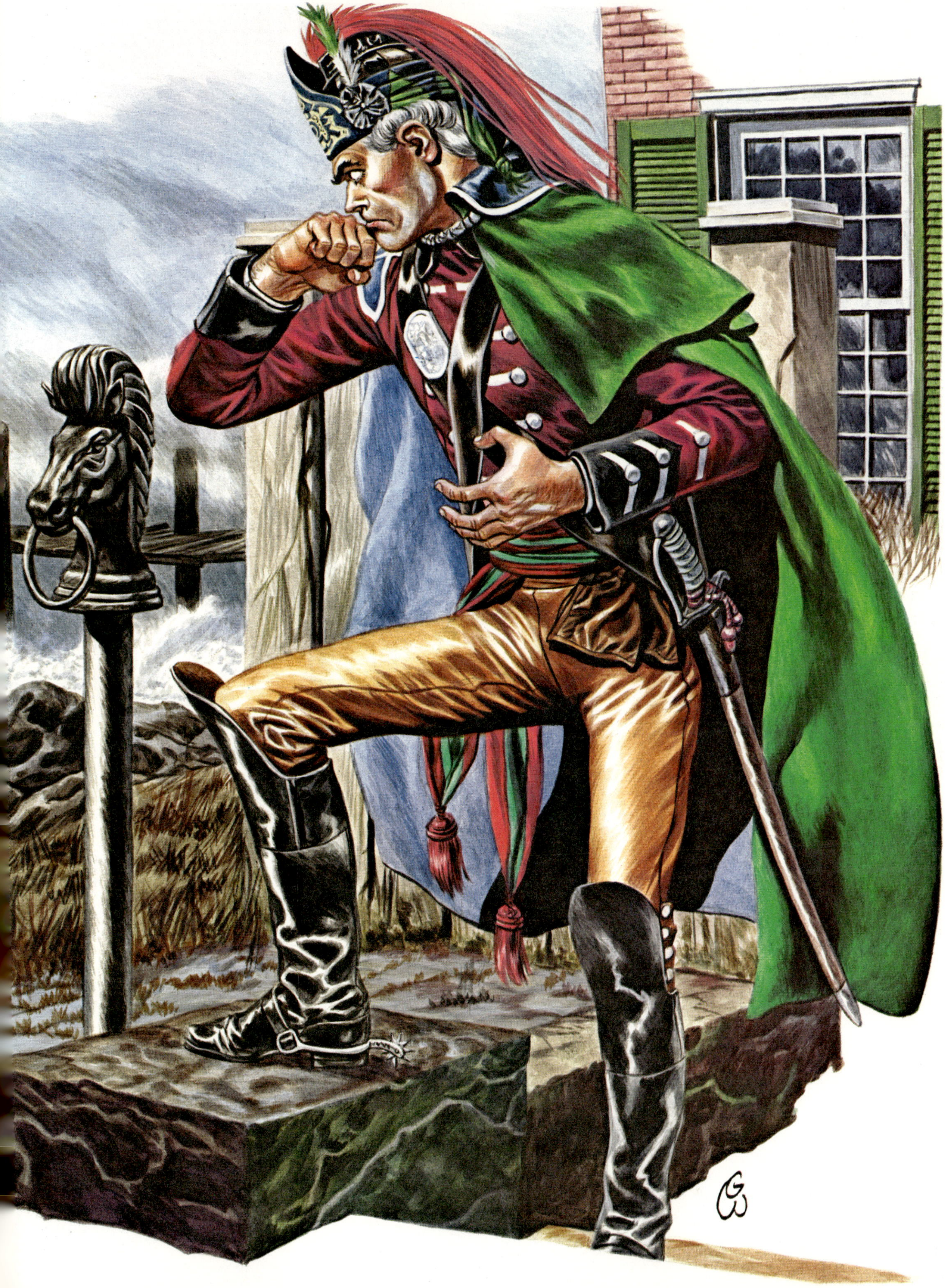

THE SPONTANEOUS HEROES

Those new states forced to fight their way into existence are apt to find that their basic civilian manpower has military faults as well as virtues. In the early part of a revolution, the citizen, highly motivated, can be depended upon to perform beyond expectations.

However, as the conflict wears on, the original, enthusiastic volunteers, decimated by casualties and other forms of attrition, are reduced below an effective level. Because of this, plus the spread of the conflict, additional units must be raised. These replacements have had the opportunity to observe the harsh reality of war. They are inclined to be somewhat more reluctant to indulge in rash heroics.

The American commanders had been made painfully aware of this fact at an early stage of the rebellion. There were never enough seasoned Continentals and, in one engagement after another, the locally called up militia had proved unreliable. Washington's generals had become exceedingly crafty in arranging their orders of battle with a view to protecting their veteran regulars from being overrun when the militia bolted in terror.

☆☆

General Daniel Morgan was a sly man. After a lifetime spent outwitting the Indians' irregular combat tactics and intimidating the fractious frontier riflemen he'd commanded earlier in the Revolution, he was not about to have his current military intentions upset by a mob of nervous rustics.

With General Nathanael Greene commanding, Washington had sent what veteran officers he could spare from watching General Clinton's British main force, to rebuild the American war effort in the southern colonies. They didn't have much to work with; a handful of Continentals, some experienced Virginia veterans and the rest, raw recruits piped with a mixture of threats and promises out of their home valleys in the hill country.

Now, Morgan with six hundred men of doubtful quality, was about to stand and face Cornwallis's deadly raider, Colonel Banastre Tarleton, at an open pastureland in South Carolina, known locally as Cowpens. Morgan's career as a guerrilla had convinced him of the value of the unusual approach. His junior officers trusted the Old Man's battle instinct, but they were still somewhat shaken at his decision to place his militia contingent, already showing signs of hysteria, in the front rank, instead of safely off on a flank, preferably one with a broad highway to the rear. As if that weren't heresy enough, the hard-bitten Indian fighter was sympathizing with their fears in an entirely soothing manner. Most incredible of all, he'd already given them permission to retreat after firing only two volleys.

The battle began with the militia carrying out Morgan's orders to the letter. They let off two ragged volleys, then galloped off eagerly to the far side of a hill behind the Regulars' positions, covered by a charge of American cavalry. They were completely unaware that their fire had stopped a charge by the British Guards.

The Continentals held the ground with their usual competence for some time, until Tarleton was tempted to throw in his last reserve, the 71st Highlanders. Under the increased pressure from these fresh troops, the American infantry began to fall back. The American line officers were too busy with the problems on their immediate front to notice that Daniel Morgan was not with them.

Instead, he was with the militia. Surprised at finding themselves still alive, even more shocked to hear their general praise their soldierly qualities, they scarcely noticed that they were being induced to double-time back into the fight. This flattery-inspired euphoria caused them to convert their advance into a headlong charge against the flank of the Scots' regulars, just as the American dragoons, having routed the British cavalry, struck from the other side.

Tarleton and a handful of staff officers, orderlies, and the like were lucky to escape the field, leaving proud British regular regiments with their hands in the air.

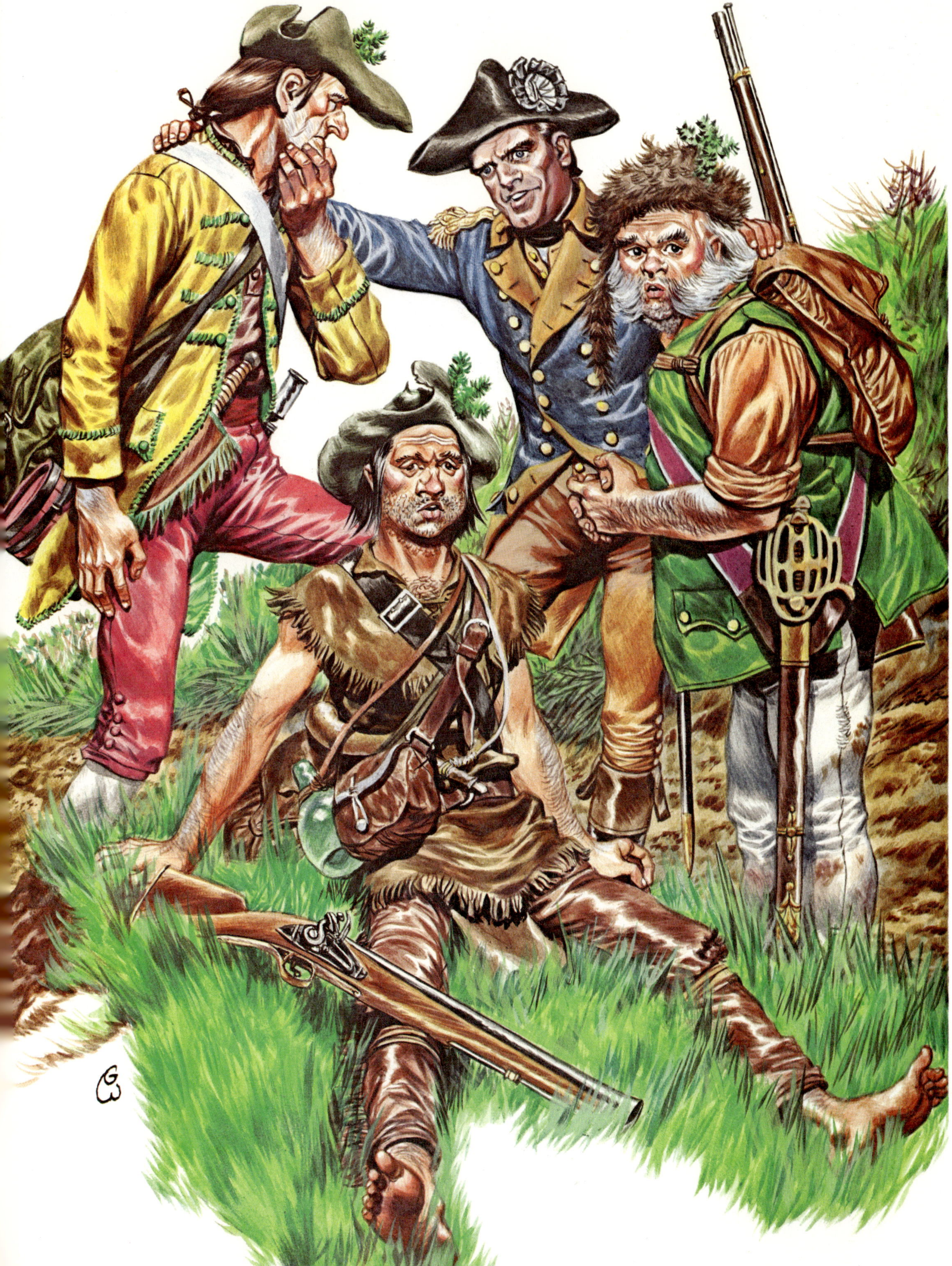

THE SMALL DESTROYERS

The exact point at which a new nation has secured its future by force of arms is often difficult to identify. Frequently, it is a series of events, some of which may even seem to be reverses at the time. But the fact that the decisive point has been passed becomes evident when the seemingly superior opponent begins making panic-prompted decisions which, in themselves, hasten the now inevitable outcome.

The permanence of the United States began to seem likely when the British shifted their attempts at suppression to the American South. The collapse of London's northern strategy at Saratoga was clearly a serious matter. How serious was masked by the continued near chaos, military and political, on the Rebel side. Washington's Army was to continue to deteriorate. Decimated by desertions, disease and casualties, on the verge of mutiny over unequal treatment, it barely survived the winter quarters following Valley Forge.

Oddly, the British seemed to lack either the power or the energy to exploit their seeming advantage. Indeed, they cautiously pulled back from the salient formed by their occupation of Philadelphia and appeared to be obsessed with improving the fortifications of New York City, their stronghold.

The decision to mount a campaign under the command of Lord Cornwallis (an energetic general) in the Carolinas and Virginia was apparently a search for a soft spot, based on the London belief that popular sentiment in that part of the rebellious colonies was still on their side. If so, their tactic of raiding and burning and their widespread use of embittered, brutal Tory troops was inept. Further, the nature of the campaigning, with its numerous small engagements and long, forced marches through rough terrain, was especially hard on troops trained for more conventional warfare.

☆☆

Colonel William Washington wished that his cousin, the commander in chief, could be on the field to witness what a deadly weapon the Continental Dragoons when properly employed, had become. At Guilford Court House, Major General Nathanael Greene had chosen a ground ideal for his purpose. The mission of this small American force was to cause attrition, to wear down the British combat spirit. In addition, Greene and his cavalry commander had an extra reason to bloody Cornwallis. The surrender of American General Lincoln's army to Clinton at Charleston had almost obliterated any pretense of a Southern Department in the Continental Army.

The battle had begun with a heavy cavalry skirmish. The British had suffered. "Light-Horse Harry" Lee's Virginia Horse had ambushed the hated Tory Cavalry of Colonel Tarleton's British Legion, destroying their effectiveness. The North Carolina militia had proved more reliable than anticipated. The Virginians were fighting well and, as always, the unflappable Delaware and Maryland Continentals were inflicting massive damage. The British and Hessians had faltered and into the melee had ridden Washington's Dragoons. A shaken Cornwallis had ordered his artillery to open fire at point-blank range on the swirling mass of men and horses, Royalist and Rebel alike.

Greene knew now that he had accomplished his purpose. To continue the fight would only cost casualties in return for ground he was not strong enough to hold. The American bugles and drums passed the word to withdraw and the American units began pulling out. Cornwallis made no attempt to interfere. It would be a crippled army he would now lead fatefully to a tobacco port called York Town.

My Lord Cornwallis's dispatches to London claiming a victory were to be the subject of some sardonic humor among the wits of the British drawing room set.

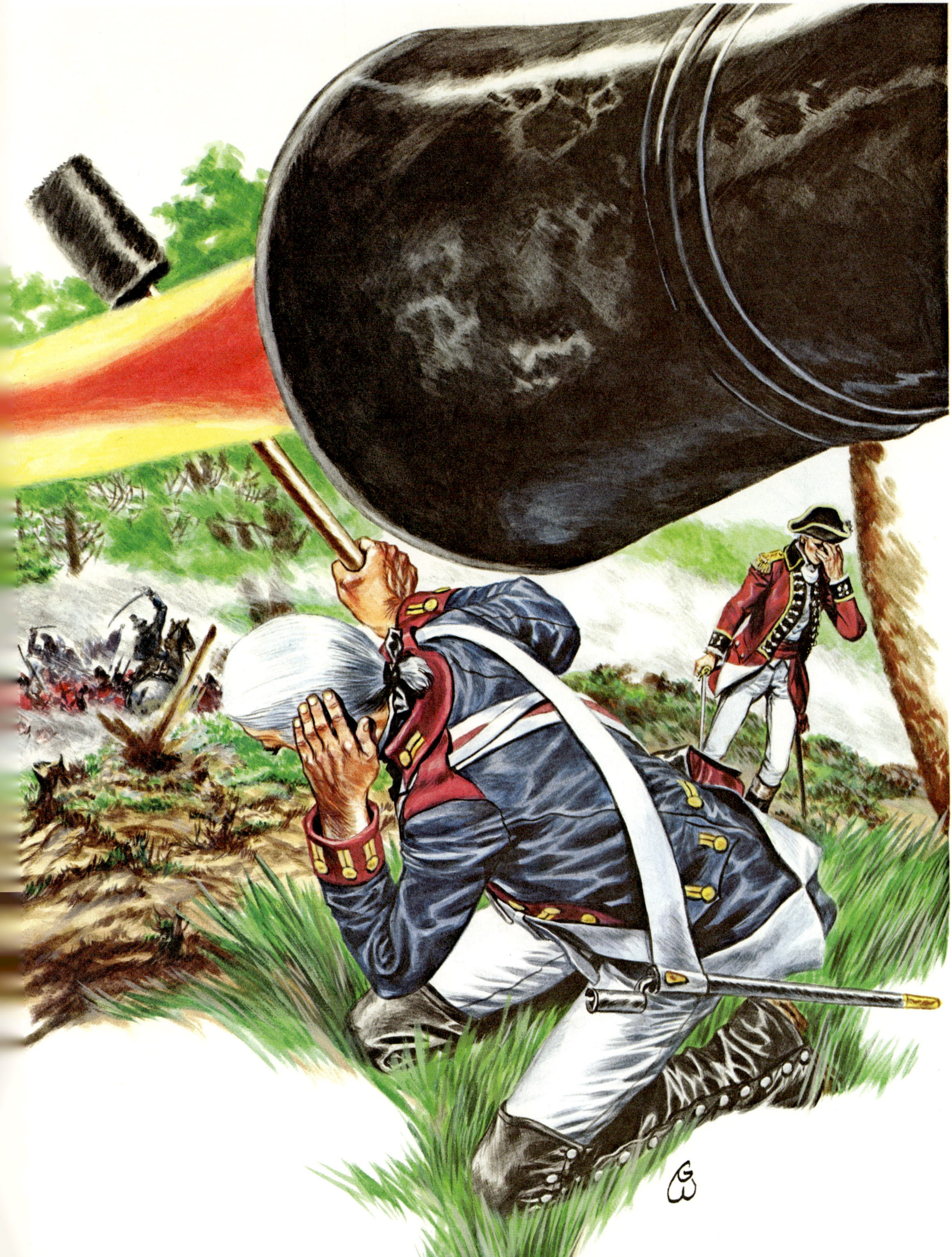

THE NIGHT RIDER

In any new government, the responsible leadership is bound to be thinly spread. Losing the services of any part of that leadership can be a crippling blow to a hastily assembled political structure.

Throughout the American Revolution, it was a recurring dream of the more melodramatic British captains that one day they would round up a key gaggle of Rebel instigators, leaving the mutinous masses of followers milling around in hopeless confusion. The American authorities were aware of the danger, but the imperatives of threshing out, in person, the myriad problems, civil and military, of a new government attempting to create itself while fighting a major war made the risks unavoidable.

☆☆☆

His horse was running strongly. This Albemarle County of Virginia was famous for its fine horses and Captain Jack Jouette had chosen the finest specimen of which his father's plantation could boast. He'd suspected when he joined the Rebel militia, that one day such an animal would come in handy. It had proved to be a reasonable assumption.

It had been chance that a business errand for his father had brought him to the Cuckoo Tavern the night that Colonel Banastre Tarleton's raiding party had ridden by on the Charlottesville road. Under Lord Cornwallis and General Benedict Arnold, the British Army had been burning and looting throughout this part of the South with ugly efficiency. The sight of one of their punitive columns on the road was not a rare sight, but Jack Jouette realized that this one had to be different.

Prudence had dictated that the American militiaman find a hideout at the first sound of approaching cavalry on the road. From a convenient closet, he'd overheard enough to enable him to realize their mission. Evidently there had been a leak in Virginia security. Somehow Banastre Tarleton knew that at Charlottesville were gathered some of the men most important to the American cause in the South. Thomas Jefferson, Patrick Henry, Richard Henry Lee, Thomas Nelson, Jr., Benjamin Harrison: the capture of these men would deal yet another blow to the decimated leadership in the South; might indeed place the Revolution itself in hazard.

Now Jouette spurred his horse recklessly along back trails known only to the local people. The track was a mere trace, almost invisible in the night. Low-hanging, interlaced branches masked the way. Only the most sure-footed horse could make any time at all over such treacherous underfooting. The Virginian had no choice. Tarleton's troop was on the high road, riding hard.

Now Jouette's horse was splashing across a shallow stream, Rivanna River and its ford near Milton. The horse was beginning to tire. The rider eased the pace as much as he dared. Just a few more miles. He risked a quick glance at his watch. Four-thirty in the morning. It would be light in another hour. Softly, the militiaman murmured words of encouragement into his horse's ear. The animal responded like the thoroughbred he was. There were lights in the cookhouse behind the elegant mansion when the tired horse and rider halted before its columned portico. The big house was still asleep. Jouette pounded urgently on its door with his saber hilt.

Then there was a scurrying of servants, still half asleep, the sound of voices calling, ordering. Half-dressed grooms came, leading riding horses and bringing carriages. Jouette leaned wearily against a door, listened to the sounds of hasty departures. Then there was a word of thanks, a quick handshake from a tall, red-haired man, a chorus of farewells.

And miles away, "Butcher" Tarleton was still breakfasting at Doctor Thomas Walker's home, Castle Hill, unaware that Thomas Jefferson and his colleagues would not be his involuntary guests this time.

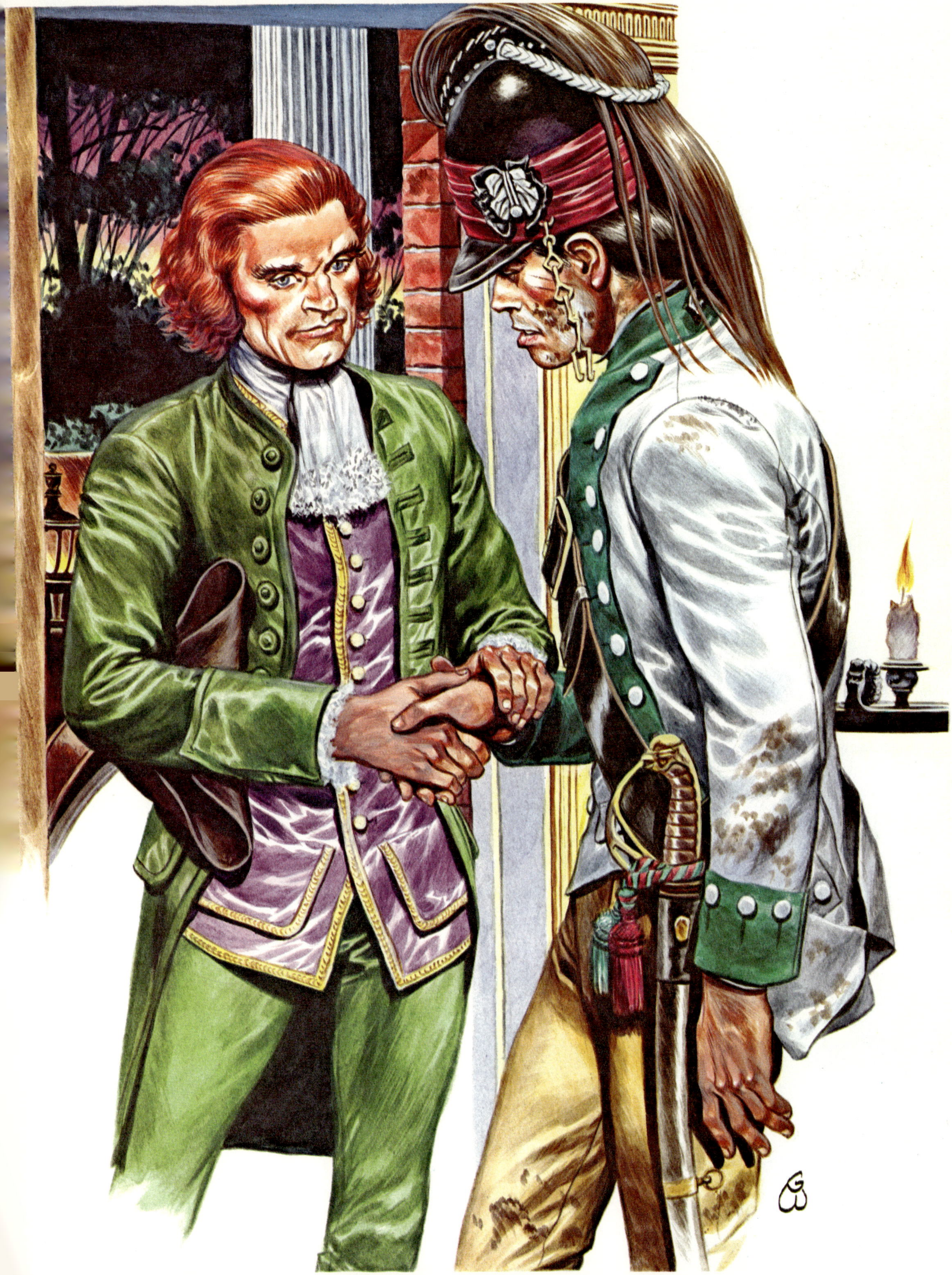

THE MUTINEERS

To the commanders of a revolutionary army, the possibility of mutiny is a harsh reality which must always be regarded as a threat. The threat becomes greater as the revolt drags on. The gradual waning of expectations of victory, the failure of an amateurish supply system because of short funds, inefficiency, and the corruption of venal contractors; inequalities of pay and treatment, and extra hazards forced on the veteran units which, because they have already done more than their share, can be depended upon. All these factors were very much present in the Continental Army after over six years of hard, often futile, campaigning and unfulfilled promises. Under the system arrived at by Congress, the several states were responsible for raising and equipping their share of the regiments in the Continental Line. As time passed and opinion varied, the individual states found it necessary to offer whatever inducements of pay, bonuses, and length of service that would seem the most attractive to potential recruits. As the inducements became greater, so did the resentment of the veterans who'd enlisted earliest and for the duration, with little or no bounty. When, in addition, there was an almost complete failure of the food and clothing supply system in the middle of the most brutal winter of all, mutiny in the American Army was almost inevitable.

☆☆☆

When it came, ironically, it was one of the proudest brigades in the Continental Line which turned out its officers. "Mad Anthony" Wayne's Pennsylvania Line was one of the best. What they did would today be more aptly called a "job action." The troops had forced their commissioned officers, sometimes by force, out of the camp. Then, oddly enough, they'd maintained discipline of a sort, appointing committees of sergeants to take command and to compose a statement of grievances to be submitted to the Congress in Philadelphia.

The British had attempted to capitalize on the situation, by sending in Tory agents, with instructions to flatter, bribe, and otherwise lure the mutineers into taking the King's shilling. These agents had been savagely manhandled. In the end, after much proposal and counterproposal, the Pennsylvanians had submitted. Faced with the prospect of having loyal Continentals sent to disarm them, they'd been unwilling to exchange fire with their own comrades-at-arms.

Now, still sullenly resentful, but again under General Wayne's orders, they were being force-marched southward into Virginia. They were still very much in disgrace, with their weapons and ammunition traveling separately, under guard. Use of this weaponry was necessary at an action which promised to be of some importance.

An opportunity had come about, as such things sometimes do in war, out of the blue. After a series of pointless skirmishes with American forces under the Marquis de Lafayette and the Baron von Steuben, Lord Cornwallis had elected to pull back to the coast in order to keep open his sea communications with General Clinton in New York. He'd chosen as his base the Virginia tobacco port of Yorktown. Then, Generals Washington and Rochambeau, watching Clinton in New York, had received word that a large French fleet, under the Count de Grasse, was at sea and available to blockade Cornwallis' sea lanes, out of Chesapeake Bay. It was a classic strategic situation. Washington acted upon it. He sent his combined corps of French and Americans (including Wayne's Pennsylvanians) south to close the trap.

Watching his grim-faced, sullen ex-mutineers swing by, Wayne could sense their anger and frustration. "Mad Anthony" was pleased. The Pennsylvanians would take out their bad temper on the first available target. Lord Cornwallis and his British and Royalist troops were to find that they were face to face with a body of very mean Americans.

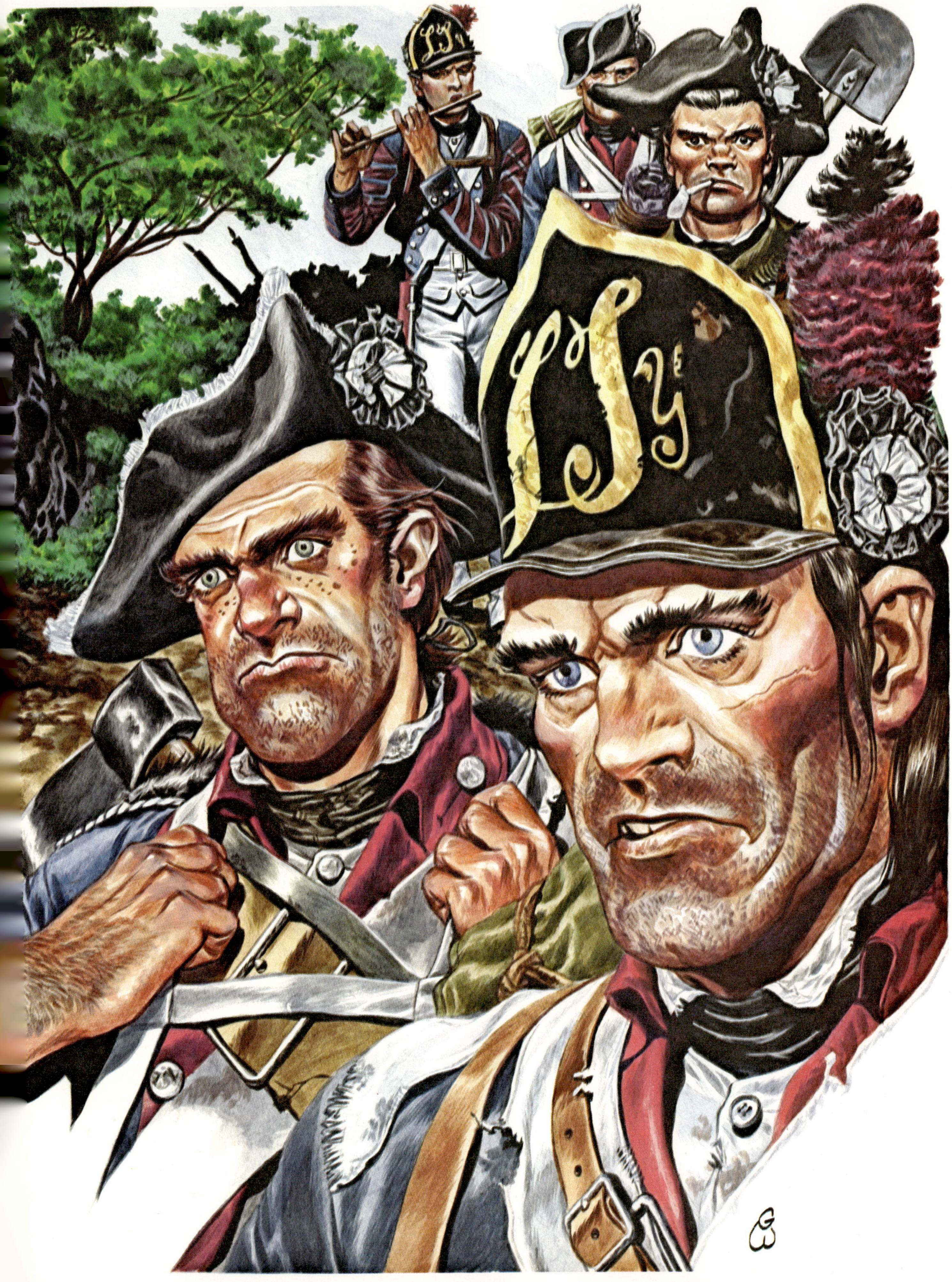

THE MISSIONARY

The plight of a new-born state, clumsily trying to liberate itself from a powerful empire, is bound to arouse the sympathies of the world's idealists. From the ranks of those moved deeply enough and eager to become involved, come the volunteers who find their ways to the arenas where freedom is at stake.

The American rebellion attracted more than its share. From France, in particular, came large numbers of young men, mostly from the aristocracy and the bourgeoisie, educated and committed to the ideas of Rousseau and Voltaire, ready to convert theory to reality. Often enough, both military and civilian, they were "Gentleman Volunteers," without orders, holding no posts and paying their own way.

☆☆☆

The assault on the twin key redoubts anchoring Lord Cornwallis's lines outside Yorktown was bound to be a bloody business, the sort where a man could gain fame and glory, if he survived. The volunteers were enthusiastically determined to participate. Both Colonel Alexander Hamilton, commanding the American assault team assigned to take the "Rocky Redoubt," and the Count Deuz-Ponts of the Gatinois Regiment, whose objective was #9 redoubt, were besieged by young Frenchmen who had not been detailed to the strike by Generals Washington or Rochambeau.

Colonel Hamilton's Continentals took their objective in a short, vicious fight. The French found theirs a bit more formidable. Their pioneers had been forced to hack a way through a labyrinth of an abatis before the infantry could scale the walls. It was during this delay that the bulk of the French casualties occurred. Then, they'd been through it and swarming over the walls, to be met by a desperation charge by the Hessian defenders. There was a wild melee for a few moments in the constricted space; then the fight was over. The surviving Germans either surrendered or fled toward doomed Yorktown.

The young Count de Damas ignored his wound. It seemed odd that it would be here, in this shattered fortification, smelling of spent powder and filled with the aftersounds of battle, that the long fight for liberty was realized. It was precisely the situation. The siege camp had known for a long time that Cornwallis could not hold out indefinitely and that no relief force could arrive in time. With his surrender, the British occupying army was broken. It was now a matter for the politicians to settle.

These remarkable Americans would be free men, living proof that the rigid structure of a class society could be dismantled. Surely then, if the Americans could do it, why not the Frenchmen whose intellectuals were already so deeply involved with the concept of democracy? An aristocrat himself, Monsieur de Damas was convinced that the republican ideals he and his friends would take back with them would quickly sweep France.

He could not see what an ironic twist history had in store for him. A decade later, revolution would indeed sweep France and he would find himself at the head of a troop of cavalry, escorting a convoy of coaches at breakneck speed through the town of Varennes on the way to the frontier. The haste was imperative. In the carriages were Louis XVI, King of France, and his queen, Marie Antoinette, fleeing the Paris mob already drunk with power and the obscenity of the guillotine. De Damas was to learn that revolutions were not by their nature self-governing. His revolt of the French would run wild. Its early leaders—reasonable, responsible men—would be pushed aside, even murdered, by radical demagogues, ever more debased, until the mob itself became king.

Shocked by the Revolution's violent course, he'd be among those who'd try to maintain some semblance of decent order during the transfer of power. For this reason he, with a few others, would try to save the Royal Family from the sans-culottes. Then, in the provincial town, it would happen. An excited crowd blocking the street, his order to his troopers to clear the way ignored; the convoy would be turned back toward Paris. In a forlorn attempt to shield the queen from indignity, he would try to push back the peasants crowding around her carriage, only to be pulled from his horse, beaten and left for dead in the muddy road.

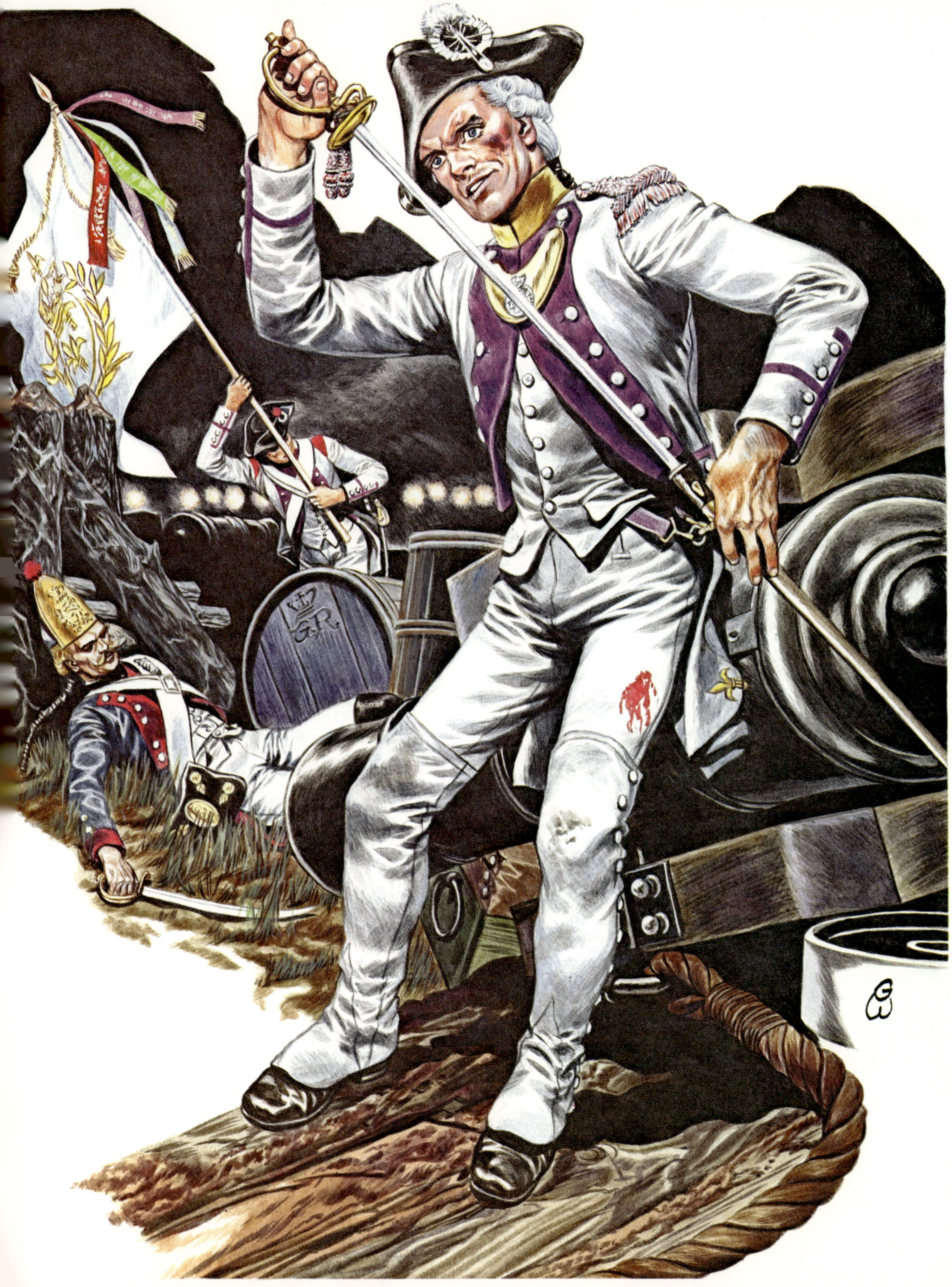

THE OLD SOLDIER

They give an army its character. Only experience can produce them, and very little of their battle wisdom comes from manuals. They are the survivors of long campaigns and bloody battles, of forced marches and endless waits. These are the noncoms, the noncommissioned officers who make up the core of any military unit. They are part of the common soldiery in everything but responsibility. They insure that the men in ranks are fed and sheltered as well as the fortunes of war will permit. They cause him to regret a slovenly appearance, or weapons not in good order. They drill him in discipline and don't expect that he will live up to their expectations. They comment on his shortcomings in language which has been gathering color and pungency since the days of the Roman legions; then, when he's overestimated his capacity for distilled spirits, they employ remarkable expedients to keep him out of the hands of the provost marshal. By their example they inspire terrified recruits to stand and fight and, often enough, restrain their superiors from making disastrous mistakes. A wise company commander will cherish a good sergeant above all the pearls in the Indies.

In seven years of continuous campaigning against the formidable regiments of the British Empire, the Continental Line of the United States Army had developed some hard-bitten specimens.

It required an effort for Sergeant Joseph Plumb Martin, Corps of Engineers, Sappers, and Miners, to remember accurately what being a civilian had been like. It seemed like several lifetimes ago that a fast-talking recruiter had convinced a bemused adolescent that a few months—six at the most—of sweeping terrified Englishmen before him, would be followed by a triumphant return home in a splendid uniform guaranteed to reduce the nubile female population of Milford, Connecticut, to ecstatic surrender. That had been up north, in the early days of the rebellion. He'd been trailing a musket and humping a pack over the muddy roads and tangled forests of these new United States ever since. He'd been in most of the major fights and had long since neglected to keep track of the number of skirmishes.

Most of the men he'd begun his soldiering with in the Fifth Connecticut had long since disappeared. He could remember most of their faces, but had long since forgotten the names. Maybe that was why he'd liked transferring out of the infantry and into the engineers. That, along with his promotion, had happened sometime after Princeton. It had been a long road which had led here to the trenches surrounding Yorktown.

He knew now that it was almost over. The goddamned British Army was bottled up in that town of York. There was water on three sides and Washington's main force, with an army of Monsoors, on the other. What's more, the warships off in the distance, blockading, were Frenchies for a change. It would take a more clever man than that Lobsterback general, Lord Cornwallis, to slip out of this one. And every night, his squad of sappers pushed their network of trenches closer to the last British lines. The no-man's-land between the lines was down to a few yards now.

It was growing light now. Behind him, Sergeant Martin could hear the faint sounds as a company of infantry quietly moved into the newly dug trench they would use as a firing position during the coming day.

Then, he saw the boy. Instinctively, he grasped his musket and snapped it to his shoulder. Then he relaxed and growled an order to the men around him. He found he was scarcely breathing. The boy stood on top of the earthwork, staring across the intervening space at the fortifications of earth and timber from which death had rained on him and his comrades for so many days. Then, he bent down. Someone out of sight passed him his drum.

With meticulous attention to the prescribed ritual for drummers as detailed in British Army drill regulations, he began a long drum roll. The sergeant looked back at his men. They returned his stare, oddly uncertain expressions on their faces. He was one of the real veterans. He'd been through it all. He was to be respected, held in awe. He would know what this meant. Martin turned back toward the British lines again. Now there was a scarlet-clad officer standing alongside the drummer. He was waving a white handkerchief.

As the sergeant watched, an American officer climbed out of the trench next door and walked slowly toward the English lines. The sergeant leaned back against the dirt wall and closed his eyes. It was finished and he was still only twenty-three.

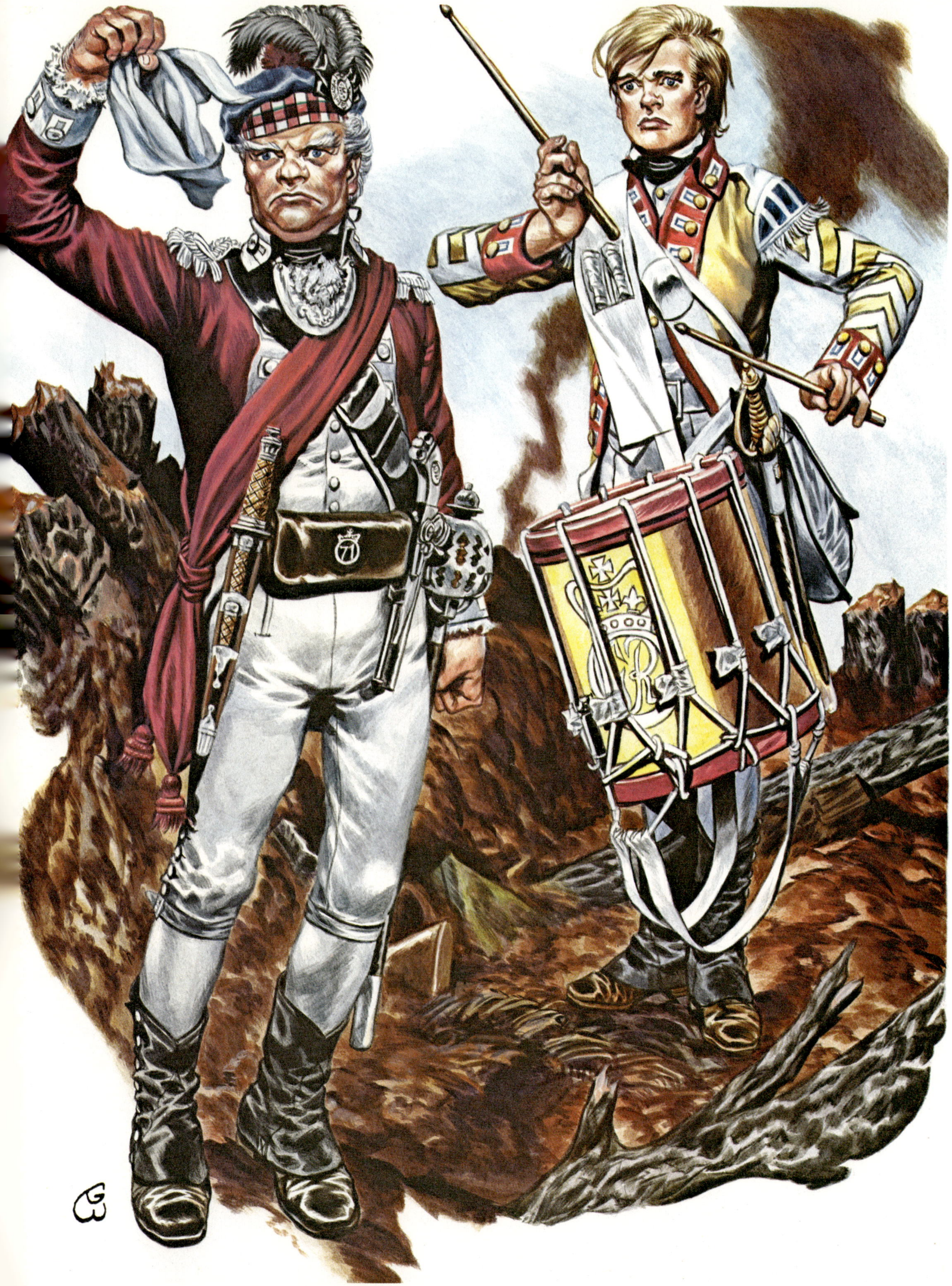

THE VICTORS

It has undoubtedly been true ever since there have been wars of liberation. As long as the issue is in doubt, patriots can ignore their differences and unite in their common, overriding aim, victory. Once that aim is achieved, however, an emerging nation must face a fateful decision. Who shall govern? Who shall shape the nation's future? Can it be welded into a viable society?

To the United States, freshly born of its revolution, the need to reach an accommodation on this vital point had suddenly become urgent.

☆☆☆

Someone had miraculously produced captured British regimental standards and draped them from the rafters. Torn, faded, and battle-stained, they still made a rich glow of color against the smoke-darkened ceiling. There was a comfortable dimness in the common room of Fraunces' Tavern. For once, the assembled men, all finally wearing the proper uniform authorized for officers in the military service of the United States, were relaxed and jovial. Still there was a sad note to this historic occasion.

There had already been high drama. In the morning, the last of Sir Henry Clinton's garrison had evacuated New York by boat for Staten Island. There, they would, with the thousands of Tory men, women and children under their protection, board the Royal Navy transports making ready for the North Atlantic crossing.

As the last scarlet jackets disappeared, a force of Americans, light infantry of the Continental Army, seven hundred men, almost all that was left of the armed forces, except for Greene's mop-up operation in the South, had moved cautiously down Broadway, alert for sniping by stray, suicidal Tories. Behind them, General Washington and Governor Clinton of New York, with their staffs, had walked their horses slowly down the same cobbled street.

Here, in the tavern, Washington bade farewell to his comrades in arms. These men had accomplished so much together. These men, more accustomed to roaring commands above the thunder of cannon, found themselves singularly inarticulate, but their feelings were obvious.

In a corner of the room, Colonel Alexander Hamilton watched. Washington had spoken simply and with dignity. To his aide-de-camp, it was evident that he was tired. That damned responsibility for so long!

Hamilton had said his farewells to his commander in chief earlier. It had been a depressing experience. Washington seemed intent on getting back to his wife and his estate in Virginia. But then, who would keep the high flame of the Revolution alive? Who would keep the greedy, the corrupt (even now plotting for power), from destroying what the men in this room had built?

He knew that most of these officers had been present in the Verplankt House, up the Hudson in Fishkill, a couple of months earlier, to lay the foundations of an order of senior military officers to be called the Society of the Cincinnati. Within that order would be the best, the noblest, the strongest men America had produced. A natural elite!

Hamilton had always been sensitive to that gulf which separated the gentlemen from the common men. Who would be better equipped to guide the new nation? These men, or the politicians in Congress?

There would be problems, of course. The people, having overthrown the British, would not be eager to place themselves under a new aristocracy, but that could easily be overcome. Standing nearby was the man every American revered, would accept unquestioningly. After all the emphasis on democracy, it would be a shock, but would there be real opposition to another royal George? It would be a constitutional monarchy, naturally. That would insure that power was in the hands of worthy men.

Washington was about to leave. Hamilton knew that discreet overtures had been made to him by the more monarchal-minded officers. It was impossible to guess what answer lay behind Washington's impassive face. He'd accepted the chair of President-General of the Society. Was that an indication?

The colonel bristled. There in the doorway was one of the most vulgar of the politicians, one who would prostitute the nation. The fellow's background was as devious as his career. He had turned up in the army in the early years, gotten himself into trouble, then managed to turn up as a lawyer and rabble-rouser here in New York. Instinctively, Alexander Hamilton disliked Aaron Burr intensely.

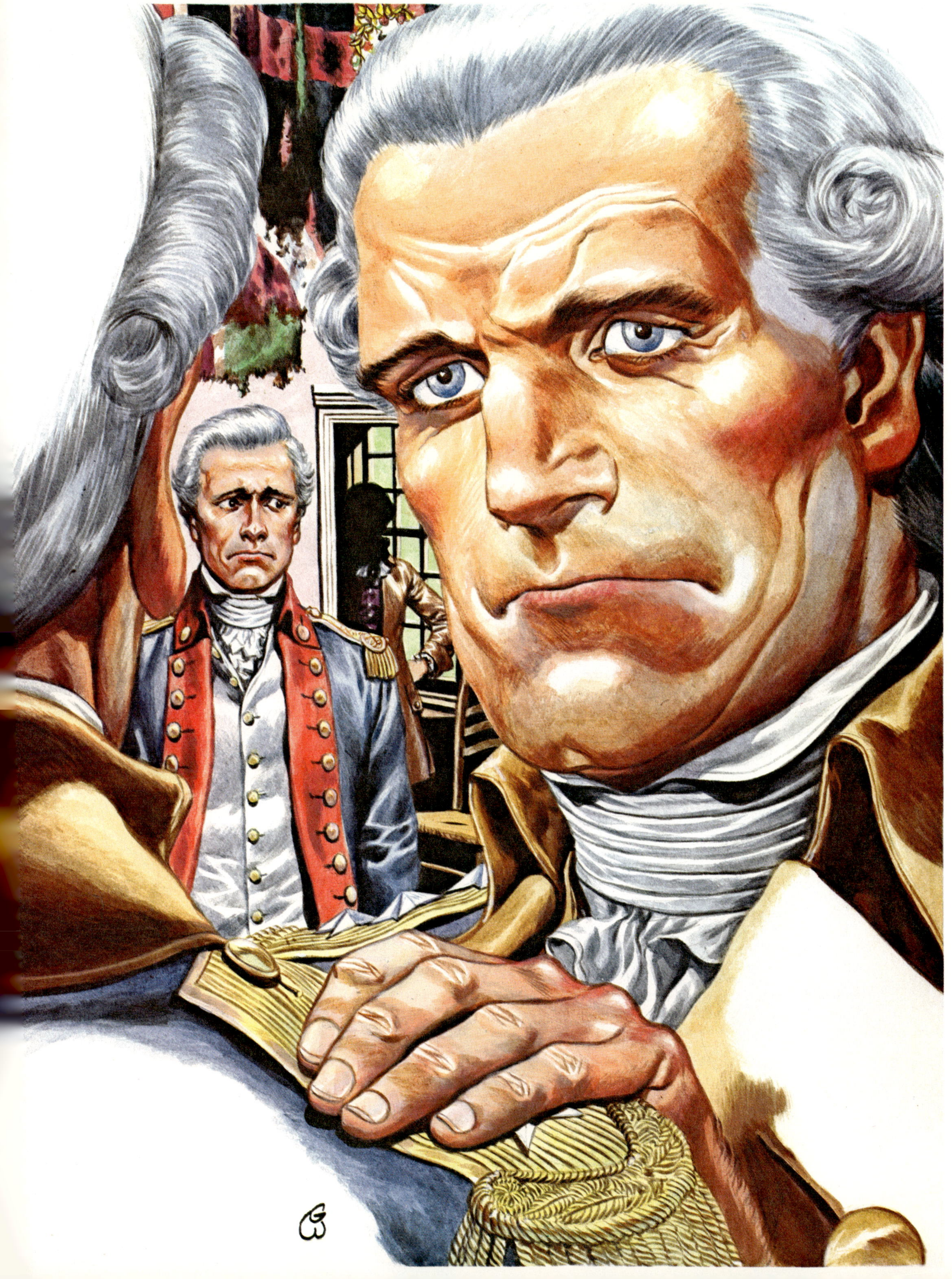

THE REACTIVATED CIVILIAN

There is often an awkward moment for the new nation, fresh from a successful revolution. It is the problem of what to do with its heroes. History is quite clear on the matter. The men who fought the revolution are not necessarily the best men to dominate the new government. The skills they have acquired in the process of establishing its freedom are usually violent ones. The ability to aim a twelve-pounder with the wizardry necessary to dismast a frigate in a heavy sea, or to plan a successful ambush of an enemy search-and-destory patrol on a moonless night, is of little use in the day-to-day functioning of a republic dedicated to peace and commerce.

Not only are these technicians of the smoking pistol and the bloody blade no longer necessary to society's survival, but they are an acute embarrassment. It is now time for another army to emerge. It is time for the bureaucrat, that indispensable priest of the establishment, to interpret the obscure subtleties of the law, to inscribe with copper-plate penmanship those imposing documents, the lists of taxpayers.

The Congress and the state legislatures of the United States faced this problem. Some of the active Rebels would automatically be drawn into the government. Soldiers like Washington and Hamilton, firebrands like Patrick Henry, theorists like Franklin, Jefferson, and Adams, would find their places in the nation's power structure. The rest, the common soldiery, these must be quickly disbanded. No new, insecure government can be easy with a victorious military force, without a further objective and with time on its hands, in its midst.

The time had definitely come to dismiss the national heroes with the heartfelt thanks of a grateful people. Of course, in case the heroes should regard this action as being slightly curt, there should be some tangible expression of the people's regard for the courage, the years of service, and the suffering. For a penniless republic, cash bonuses would be trivial at best, but the alternatives of promises and land seemed more imposing and comfortably remote. The only immediate expense involved would be the hire of sufficient printing presses to spew out the bales of scrip.

And so the Continental Army furled its battle standards and went home.

☆☆☆

The man in the shabby blue regimentals was obviously a veteran of the Regular Line. He swung along the muddy dirt road with the easy, distance-consuming gait of the infantryman. His gear had the look of long use and diligent care. He carried no excess baggage. His name didn't matter. He was one of thousands of common soldiers going home on roads like this one which led to a thousand towns and farms.

A lifetime ago, the traffic over this nameless pike had been all in the opposite direction. It had begun with an itinerant peddler, with copies of the city papers in his pack. The columns had told of the revolt of the people of Boston, of the gathering of militia troops from all the colonies to besiege the British. Most of the able-bodied men had begun walking toward Boston. The ex-soldier didn't know if any of the others would be coming back. He and his friends had become separated somewhere in the confusion, the battles, the marches, the endless regrouping of shattered regiments. He considered it remarkable that he had survived himself.

Most of the men in his regiment had felt the same. And they'd been bitter, as well. The scrip they'd been issued had been the subject of grim humor. Still, in every town he'd passed through, there had been men, lawyers, merchants, smooth city men, all eager to buy up the land scrip. The old infantryman considered that interesting. It had prompted him to keep his own. After all, he'd made considerable of an investment in this republic thing they were talking about. Seven years of his life made quite an investment. A prudent man guarded his investments. In time, they could be expected to show a profit.

The old Continental paused at the crest of a hill. In the valley beyond, he could see the rooftops of the place he called home. He was completely unaware that for the last several miles he had been thinking like any other civilian.

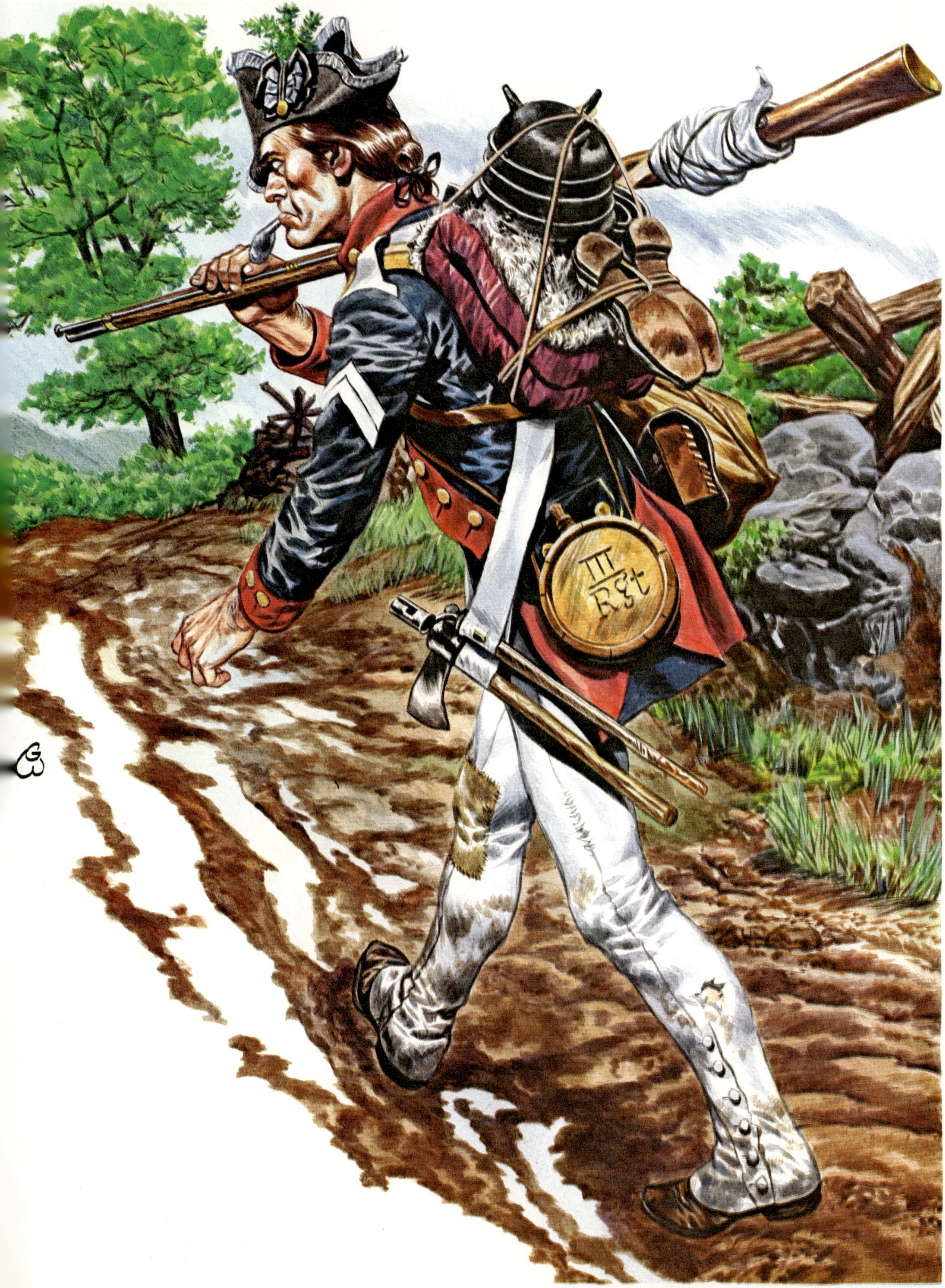
III
Rgt

INDEX

(*Note:* Page numbers in italics refer to illustrations.)

Adams, John *14*
Adams, Samuel 14
Allen, Ethan 22
Ancrum, Maj. *44*
André, John 76
Andros, Thomas *62*
Arnold, Benedict 22, 44, 52, 76, 78, 84

Barton, William *34*
"Battle of the Kegs" 54
Baum, Friedrich 46
Beaumarchais, Pierre A. C. de 42
Bemis Heights, Battle of 52
Bennington, Battle of 46
Brant, Joseph 68
Breed's Hill, Battle of 20
Breymann, Heinrich von 46
Burgoyne, John 46, 52
Bushnell, David *54*
Butler, John 68
Butler, Richard 66

Chadd's Ford 48
Champe, John *78*
Clark, George Rogers 64
Clinton, George 50
Clinton, Henry 50, 68
Cornwallis, Charles 30, 82, 86
Cowpens, Battle of 80
Culper, Jr. 76

Damas, Count de 88
Darrah, Lydia *58*
Dawes, William 12
Deane, Silas *42*
Delaplace, William 22
Deuz-Ponts, Count William *88*
Dring, Thomas 62

Estaing, Hector d'

Francisco, Peter 48
Franklin, Benjamin 42, 56
Fraunces' Tavern *8*, *24*, *92*

Gates, Horatio 52, 74
Glover, John *40*
Graaff, Johannes de *32*
Grasse, Count de 48
Greene, Nathanael 30, 82
Guilford Court House, Battle of 82

Hamilton, Alexander 56, 88, 92
Hamilton, Henry 64
Hamilton, William *72*
Hancock, John 14
Harrington, Mrs. Jonathan *16*
Hawkins, Christopher 62
Helms, Leonard *64*
Hill, Hugh *26*
Holbrook, Abraham 12
Honeyman, John *38*
Hopkinson, Francis 54
Howe, Sir William 24, 48, 58

Iroquois 44, 68

Jameson, John 76
Johnson, Lt. Col. 66
Jones, John Paul 72
Jouette, Jack *84*

Knox, Henry 22, *24*, 40
Knyphausen, Wilhelm von 30
Kosciusko, Thaddeus 52

Lafayette, Marquis de 48
Lee, Charles 34, 60
Lee, "Light-Horse Harry" 78, 82
Lexington, Battle of 16
Lincoln, Benjamin 70

Machin, Thomas *68*
McLane, Allan *58*
Magaw, Robert *30*
Marion, Francis *74*
Martin, Joseph Plumb *28*, *90*
Montgomery, Fort 50
Morgan, Daniel 52, 80

Newton, Battle of 68

Overing, John 34

Paddock, Maj. 12
Paine, Thomas *36*
Parker, John 16
Peck, Samuel 28
Percy, Hugh 30

Pitcairn, John 16
Pixley, Ely 44
Prescott, Richard 34
Prescott, Dr. Samuel 12
Preston, Thomas 14
Prevost, Augustine 70
Pulaski, Count Casimir 70
Putnam, Israel 50

Quincy, Josiah 14

Rall, Johann 30
Revere, Paul 12, 14
Robinson, Isaiah *32*
Rochambeau, Comte de 86

St. Leger, Barry 44
Savannah, Battle of 70
Schuyler, Hon Yost 44
Schuyler, Philip 24, 46, 52
Simcoe, John G. 76
Smith, William 60
Stanwix, Fort 44
Stark, John 46
Steuben, Baron Friedrich von 56, 66
Stiles, Ely 44
Stony Point, Battle of 66
Sullivan, John 48

Tallmadge, Benjamin 76
Tarleton, Banastre 74, 80, 84
Ticonderoga, Fort 22
Townsend, Robert 76
Townsend, Sally 76
Trumbull, John *18*

Vergennes, Comte Charles de 42

Warren, Dr. Joseph 14, *20*
Washington, George 24, 56, 60, 78, 80, 86, 92
Washington, William 82
Wayne, "Mad Anthony" 48, 66, 86

Yorktown, Battle of 88, 90
Young, Capt. 62

96